History, Sociology and Education

HISTORY OF
EDUCATION SOCIETY

History, Sociology and Education

METHUEN & CO LTD
11 NEW FETTER LANE LONDON EC4

First published in 1971
by Methuen & Co Ltd
11 New Fetter Lane London EC4
© *1971 by History of Education Society*
Printed in Great Britain by
Cox & Wyman Ltd., Fakenham, Norfolk

SBN 416 66020 7

Distributed in the USA
by Barnes & Noble Inc.

Contents

68463

History of education society

Chairman | David Bradshaw
(Principal, Doncaster College of
Education)

Vice-Chairman | Professor Brian Simon
(Leicester University School of
Education)

Secretary | Ian Taylor
(St John's College, York)

Treasurer | Trevor Hearl
(St Paul's College, Cheltenham)

Editor of the Bulletin | T. G. Cook
(Cambridge University Department of
Education)

Other Committee
Members | Professor W. H. G. Armytage
(Sheffield University Department of
Education)
Professor Kenneth Charlton
(Birmingham University School of
Education)
Malcolm Seaborne
(Principal, Chester College)

Nanette Whitbread
(City of Leicester College of Education)

The aim of the Society, founded in 1967, is to further the study of the history of education by providing opportunities for discussion among those engaged in its study and teaching.

Conferences and meetings are organized, a bulletin is published twice a year in spring and autumn and other publications pertaining to the history of education are sponsored.

Membership is open to all connected in a professional capacity with education, or engaged in the study or teaching of the history of education. Overseas members are welcomed and are offered a specially reduced subscription rate. Libraries are invited to subscribe to the bulletin only; otherwise Society membership is individual not institutional.

Annual Subscriptions	Members	£2
	Overseas Members	
	(surface mail)	£1
	Student Members	50p
	Libraries	£1
Life Membership		£25

Preface

Historians have for long been aware that their discipline does not stand in isolation but draws from, and contributes to, other disciplines. Historians of education, in particular, are professionally closely involved with those teaching and researching in other disciplines and share inevitably in this awareness. Perhaps, however, in their relationships with practitioners of the social sciences there is a certain apprehension. In *Crisis in the Humanities* Professor Plumb writes, 'In a sense the social sciences are fighting for life, the humanities against death.' Though the History of Education Society is of recent foundation, the study of history of education has itself a respectably lengthy past. Concerned for a great while with the pioneering activities and writings of individual educators and then with the legal and constitutional framework on which our present educational system was constructed, historians of education are now increasingly addressing themselves to education as an activity of men in society. In this way historians and sociologists come to be surveying the same or similar fields, yet each discipline appears to have its own aims and techniques. It is therefore necessary for the historian to enquire what methods the sociologist is using and what ends he is pursuing. Does it follow from Professor Plumb's statement that sociology is one of the youthful social sciences on which a moribund study of history may draw for rejuvenation?

The purpose of the Society's Conference held at Nottingham in December 1970 was to engage in an enquiry into the relationships between the history and sociology of education by inviting notable practitioners of sociology to discuss the aims and methods of their discipline and to demonstrate these methods in operation in historical situations. This collection of papers begins with a contribution from Gerald Bernbaum of the University of Leicester who considers broadly the sociologist's methods and techniques, placing them in the context of historical study and seeking to 'demonstrate how they have been, or might be, used to benefit the historian's examination of the past'.

In subsequent papers further demonstrations of the applications of these techniques are given. Professor Kelsall of the University of Sheffield considers the methods of recruitment to the higher civil service in Britain, showing how selection, based on written competitive examinations, was affected by the introduction of the interview in the period between the First and Second World Wars. Professor Musgrove of the University of Manchester seeks to deal with the question of power and authority in Victorian schools in order to throw light on his investigation of bureaucratic tendencies in present-day internal school organization.

The last paper in this collection, by Professor Kenneth Charlton, of the University of Birmingham, analyses elements in the present relationship of the disciplines of history and sociology and, in particular, examines claims which sociologists have made for the application of their techniques to the study of the past. This leads him to consider the fundamental question of the differing nature of the two disciplines. We hope that this volume as a whole will contribute to the continuing discussion of this important theme.

Thanks to the agreement of our speakers and the willingness of Messrs Methuen and Co to undertake publication, the Society is again fortunate in being able to publish the papers of its annual conference. We have been encouraged in this by the success of the previous volumes, *Studies in the Government and Control of Education* (1970) and *The Changing Curriculum* (1971).

The Society is grateful to Professor Charlton for his preparatory editorial work and to Miss Hebe Jerrold for compiling the index.

T. G. Cook

University of Cambridge

GERALD BERNBAUM

Sociological techniques and historical study

The purpose of this paper is to examine some of the methods and
techniques which are employed by sociologists, to place them in the
context of historical study and to demonstrate how they have been,
or might be, used to benefit the historian's examination of the past.
In doing this I had hoped to be able to move away from a discussion
about the nature of the two disciplines, and concentrate more immediately on the practical task that is embodied in the title of the
paper. The longer I considered the presentation of the material, however, the greater became my conviction that it is impossible to separate the methods of a discipline from its nature and purposes, and
that any adequate consideration of the relevance of sociological
techniques to historical study must include a discussion of the distinctive features of the two disciplines along with the contribution
that each can make to the other.

It is clear that the present state of knowledge in both history and
sociology might encourage some greater association between the two
subjects. Amongst many sociologists there is dissatisfaction with the
extreme versions of empiricism which have become increasingly
fashionable with the advent of the sophisticated statistical techniques
made possible by advances in computer science. Indeed, the lack of a
theoretical perspective in much of this work has given rise to
Homans's comment, 'Let us make the important quantitative, and
not the quantitative important'.[1] In addition, sociologists have begun
to criticize the heavy reliance upon the survey method of enquiry,
and to emphasize its limitations in ways which are remarkably similar
to the criticisms offered by non-sociologists. Thus Cicourel[2] has
argued recently:

How the actor makes sense of his environment and constructs
courses of action over time are not issues of verification that concern the quantitative-oriented macro theorist, except as they are
squeezed into the asserted objectivity of census materials and vital
statistics. . . . In the case of surveys, the procedures are assumed to

depict the courses of action the actor would take or has taken according to the hypothetical or factual type of questions posed. How the actor interprets the stimulus question, or the possibility that the respondent's answer was motivated by the question and disengaged from his past experiences and daily activities, and thus generated 'data' relevant only to the immediate questionnaire and situation, are not matters that are more than technically problematic for this group.

It seems possible, therefore, that sociologists might well be receptive to a reminder that the early writers such as Marx, Weber, Simmel and Durkheim were noted for their use of historical perspectives, material and data in their attempts to understand the structure of societies and change within them. Moreover, it should be noted that C. Wright Mills in his book *The Sociological Imagination* has argued that 'history is the shank of social study'[3] and that 'every social science requires an historical scope of conceptions and a full use of historical materials'.[4]

Similarly, despite the protestations of Professor Elton, many historians are beginning to express doubts about certain aspects of their subject. Thus Professor Plumb has recently told us that 'placed against the obvious power and effectiveness of scientific enquiry or even economic analysis, historical generalizations must seem hopelessly tentative and jejune'[5] and that

the modern historian is crucified by this dilemma: he must act like a scientist although historical objectivity cannot exist. His work can have no validity except for himself, and perhaps for fellow historians playing the same game by the same rules or perhaps for those men of his age who think and feel like himself.[6]

In a more particular manner Lawrence Stone has declared that 'the history of education is at such a primitive stage ... both in the collection of data and the formulation of concepts, that it is impossible to provide more than tentative and provisional answers to the many problems involved.'[7]

It is interesting here to note that Professors Plumb and Stone have pitted themselves against older views of history, and choose to express themselves in terms of 'scientific enquiry', 'objectivity', 'formulation of concepts'. In this way, therefore, they appear to be seeking after some kind of sociological method, though, as has already been argued, it is impossible to consider the methods without reference to the nature of the discipline. The corollary of this argument, however, is that it is impossible to conduct the debate in terms of historians utilizing, in a haphazard fashion, a selection of techniques borrowed from the social sciences, or of sociologists culling details from the research monographs of historians with which to demonstrate the validity of their theoretical perspectives. The issue is clearly put by Mr Holloway when he writes:

> ... it is often assumed that the inadequacies of history and sociology will disappear if only historians and sociologists will talk to one another and learn to work together. This solution seems attractive because it does not disturb the present division of labour within the universities: but the truth is that the advance of both sociology and history will be held back until sociologists become historians and historians sociologists. It is not a question of sociologists talking to and working with historians: it is a matter of people trained in both disciplines taking up theory and research.[8]

In this context it is worth remembering that Alan Ryan has pointedly remarked:

> ... to worry over whether a book like Smelser's *Social Change in the Industrial Revolution* is history or sociology is plainly wrong – insofar as it applies sociological insights to the explanations of historical events it makes good history, and insofar as it uses the evidence of these events to illuminate sociological theory, it makes good sociology.[9]

Nevertheless, there remain formidable obstacles to the attainment of the real unification of the subjects. Foremost amongst these is the way in which sociologists and historians claim to see the nature of each other's subject, especially in respect of generalizations. In many ways, however, the historian's criticisms of sociology are frequently based on misconceptions of the sociological perspective, whilst the sociologist's attacks on historians frequently ignore the most recent changes which have occurred in historical scholarship.

There is not at the present time a general body of sociological theory which has been validated or widely accepted. Indeed, most modern sociologists have abandoned attempts to discover or utilize 'social laws' or to apply some kind of evolutionary or developmental conceptual framework to the history of mankind. More modestly, nowadays, sociologists have concentrated on working out precise concepts and more adequate classifications, though in this last activity they have formulated that type of limited generalization which is involved in the act of classification itself. Professor Bottomore has argued that it is in the development of concepts and schemes of classification that sociology has so far been most productive.[10] Concepts such as social structure, role, function, mobility, ideology, and so on, are used by all sociologists and form part of the tools by means of which they organize their thinking, plan their work and convey their results. Concepts and classificatory schemes distinguish and identify classes of phenomena which perhaps had not previously been considered as forming separate classes. They also serve as shorthand descriptions of phenomena and, very importantly, as instruments for further analysis. The use of publicly stated concepts is a vital part of the work of the sociologist and despite acknowledged difficulties their value can be determined by the results they yield both at an empirical and theoretical level.

It is, however, in the development of explanatory theories that the sociologist is often said to differ most from the historian. As has already been argued this does not necessarily mean constructing all-embracing theories. Rather it is likely to involve what the famous American sociologist R. K. Merton has called 'theories of the middle range'. Merton describes these as 'theories intermediate to the minor working hypotheses evolved in abundance during the day by day routines of research, and the all inclusive speculations comprising a master conceptual scheme from which it is hoped to derive a very large number of empirically observed uniformities of social behaviour.'[11] Thus it is being suggested that modern sociologists use theories which keep close to the empirical data and hence to verification, extension and modification. The sociological approach, therefore, involves assumptions and procedures which are available for discussion. By other similar studies an organized and systematic body of knowledge can be built up. As Merton has argued:

one consequence of such formalization is that it serves as a control over the introduction of unrelated, undisciplined and diffuse interpretations. It does not impose on the reader the task of ferreting out the relations between the interpretations embodied in the text. Above all, it prepares the way for consecutive and cumulative research rather than a buckshot array of dispersed investigations.[12]

It is the explanatory generalization of the sociologists to which most historians object. They would agree with Walsh's claim that historians 'are primarily occupied with individual events, and seldom give expression to truly universal conclusions'.[13] Nevertheless, it must remain doubtful whether this claim can, in fact, be maintained. Professor Hook has argued that 'every fact which the historian establishes presupposes some theoretical construction',[14] and Holloway has detailed clearly and wittily[15] the way in which historians in fact do use generalizations and apply concepts. He concludes sharply that 'the question whether the historian should generalize or not is meaningless: he has no alternative.[16] In addition, Holloway shows that by denying the use of generalization historians have drawn attention away from the fact that the generalizations employed operate at very different levels. Holloway establishes, further, that between the use of classificatory generalizations such as verbs like 'to colonize' and nouns like 'revolution' on the one hand, and the extensive generalization of the speculative philosophers of history on the other, historians customarily employ generalizations which might be comparative, structural, indicative of trends or tendencies, or even prophetic. If it can be accepted, therefore, that historians make statements summing up regularities, and persistently select facts according to some criteria of relevance, then it follows that they are likely to be testing hypotheses and modifying hypotheses to accommodate facts.

Professor Aydelotte has pointed out, however, that the trouble is that for most historians the process remains an unconscious procedure of analysis.[17] As W. I. Thomas and Florian Znaniecki wrote almost half a century ago in their classic study of *The Polish Peasant in Europe and America*:

a fact by itself is already an abstraction: we isolate a certain limited aspect of the concrete process of becoming, rejecting, at least provisionally, all its infinite complexity. The question is only whether we perform this abstraction methodically or not, whether we know what and why we accept and reject or simply take uncritically the old abstractions of common sense.[18]

In general terms the more formal approach adopted by historical sociologists is that of the hypothetico-deductive method for the formulation and testing of hypotheses. The historical sociologists differ from other sociologists in that they use as data documents and artefacts taken as indications of past events, rather than observations of people and social institutions, along with questions put to respondents at the present time. As Professor Banks has pointed out, however:

> In principle, there is no logical distinction between the two procedures, since the testing of universal explanatory generalizations can be carried out through the systematic examination of documents, artefacts, observations and questionnaire responses indiscriminately. The decision whether to use one or more kinds of data is merely a matter of convenience, although in some circumstances there may be differences in the levels of objectivity and precision which they offer.[19]

Thus far in this attempt to describe some of the distinctive features of history and sociology I have, by implication at least, made certain assumptions about the historian's work. In reality the study of the past is such a wide-ranging and multifarious activity that any sociologist who comments on it must beware that he does not present a partial picture. Ten years ago, for example, H. Stuart Hughes attacked academic history for its lack of systematic theory, conceptual apparatus and explicit procedures for interpretation.[20] Since he wrote, certain new approaches can be detected in historical scholarship. In the main these have been adopted without explicit reference to the whole apparatus of sociological theory and method; and even though they might be examples of the kind of selective co-operation which Holloway was anxious to avoid, they have nevertheless changed the complexion of much historical work.

The rapid growth of econometric history has signified a much greater concern with the position of theory in analysing the past, albeit economic theory, and with the application of sophisticated statistical techniques to the analysis of quantitative economic data. The social historians of population have recently developed theoretical perspectives and new methods which have virtually revolutionized the subject. The changes, which began in the mid-1950s, involve family reconstitution, and rely on methods which are essentially nominative rather than aggregative. The significance of these developments is best summed up by one of their leading exponents, Dr

Wrigley, when he writes that they have been of 'such importance that [they] enabled the subject to change gear. . . . As this technique and others like it have developed, the tie between population history generally and the history of the family has grown much closer.'[21] Similarly, the methods recently introduced by Professors Rudé[22] and Vincent[23] have strengthened our understanding of political and social history in eighteenth-century France and mid-nineteenth-century England.

In part, of course, these developments are inseparable from changes in the overall concern of historians. As long as historians concerned themselves primarily with the public activities of great men, then the opportunities to introduce the theories and techniques of the social sciences remained severely limited. At best, perhaps, some simple discussion of motivation in the context of psychological theories, or the dynamics of small groups. However, with the change of the historian's focus, and a greater interest in the study of the past of large numbers of people, and their social institutions, historians have inevitably come to ask themselves different questions. In attempting to answer them, historians have rediscovered the common interests they have with sociologists in a wide variety of aspects of human behaviour – marriage and the family, religious and social institutions, education, urbanization, industrialization, all may be taken as illustrations.

It is possible to argue, therefore, that though the present relationship between history and sociology may fall short of that unity desired by Mr Holloway, there are beginning to emerge a number of points of convergence. Thus for the historian, as the calling of this conference might suggest, the sociological imagination is seen not only as related to the historical imagination, but as an amplification of it. None of this is meant to imply a final evaluation, for if the interest of the sociologist is primarily in the general or recurrent features of human activity and that of the historian primarily in the specific or the unique, neither is more or less worthy as an activity. It is clear, though, that by its concepts and its methods sociology has a great deal to offer to historical study, and it is possible to suggest that at least as many historians are intrigued by the new discipline as are alienated by it. An acquaintance with sociological literature has sharpened the historian's feeling for occupational structure, social stratification, for the family and the whole kinship order, especially as it is related to economic and political power and the pattern of

B

social mobility. New significance has been given to the study of religious institutions and religious styles, to the problems of church
and sect, especially as they bear upon economic and political
conflict. At the same time there has been a redeveloped interest in the
function of ideologies, the history of acculturation and contrasting
styles of life and thought. Familiar historical concerns such as class
and status have been pursued with new methods, quantification has
been used in areas where historians were previously content to make
impressionistic generalizations and many of the generalizations have
not been able to stand the test of quantitative analysis. Indeed, the
eminent American historian Professor Hofstadter has argued that
'Probably the chief impact on historians of their increasing exposure
to sociology has been a growing awareness of the complexity of their
task and of the variety of methods available to them which hitherto
have been little used.'[24]

Given our present concerns, one of the interesting features of this
discussion of the nature of the relationship between history and
sociology is the way in which, as sociology developed, sociologists
accepted historians' methods and data as the starting-point of their
own investigations. As the new discipline has become more firmly
established, the historians increasingly want to know what the
methods of sociology have to offer. Thus, in the early discussions, the
sociologists devoted most of their time to the question of the usefulness and validity of the personal document. Indeed, a whole bulletin
of the American Social Science Research Council was given over to
the *The Use of the Personal Document in History, Anthropology and
Sociology.*[25] Nowadays, however, as the historian seeks the certainty
of social science through content analysis, we might well begin here
our more detailed discussion of methodologies. By modern standards
the discussion of the 1930s and 1940s on the question of personal
documents often seems naïve. It concentrated to a large degree on
the matter of validating documents, and on the difficulty in determining the truth of the comments. Yet it is hard to say the arguments
proceed much further than the way the issue was put at the beginning
of the century by Langois and Seignobos when they wrote 'Knowing
what the author of the document has said we ask (1) What did he
mean? (2) Did he believe what he said? (3) Was he justified in believ-
ing whatever he did believe?'[26]

Modern sociologists might employ personal documents as a

means of obtaining conceptual 'hunches', though it must be remembered that hypotheses derived from a few personal documents are likely to prove false because of the possibilities of bias or lack of objectivity in the persons whose experiences are drawn upon. It is important to recognize that the original hypothesis must be formulated in such a way that it can be refined and retested. If the researcher is not careful, enquiries by this approach too readily lend themselves to the major error of proceeding by way of hypothesis to example and then back to hypothesis again. In this context it should be recognized, also, that verification of a hypothesis and demonstration that it has been verified are not the same thing. The investigator may be satisfied that he has verified a hypothesis, but he cannot convince others of it unless he presents all the evidence, or at least enough of it so that others may see the character of the inductive check which he claims to have made. Thus in my own work on the development of the headmaster's role[27] it was hypothesized that the social origins of the Inspectorate and their social distance from the teaching profession in the early years of this century would be important determinants of the way in which the headmaster's role came to be defined in the new secondary schools of the time. Now, there is a sense in which examination of a variety of personal documents enables the hypothesis to be proved. On the other hand, other factors of a structural or contextual kind place limitations on the nature of the proof, particularly the power of the school governors and the financial standing of the school.

Though content analysis is sometimes seen as a possible way out of the historian's problems in analysing documents, it is doubtful whether it will prove to be a very great asset. The basic idea of content analysis is to place the parts of a text (words, phrases, paragraphs, etc., depending on the units chosen) in a number of predetermined categories. Content analysis, therefore, involves the ranging of all these parts in a series of pigeon-holes, and describing the text by the number of elements in each pigeon-hole. Obviously it is possible to apply quantitative techniques to documentary data by these methods. Nevertheless it should be clear that content analysis succeeds or fails by its categories. It is also apparent that the variety of categories is almost infinite and that it is nearly always possible to invent new ones for each analysis. Occasional attempts to work out general and abstract categories have not been successful. Moreover, it is very important to recognize that the method cannot be applied to all documents. A distinction must be made between documents which report facts and those which are facts. Content analysis is usually applicable to the latter and not the former. Thus, one of the most famous analyses of content is that by Lasswell[28] who examined German propaganda during the war. He compared, particularly, Nazi broadcasts and the content of newspapers published in the United States by the German American Bund. He was able to show the very close parallel between Nazi propaganda and the themes contained in the newspapers. It should be clear, though, that this does not furnish proof of collusion between the Bund and the Nazis. For this to be established documentary evidence is required of a type which is more normally the concern of the historian, say, diplomatic messages of some kind.

As I have already suggested, modern population studies are a field where sociological perspectives have aided historical interpretation. Indeed the recent transformations have been well described by Wrigley: 'Many historians are too little alive to the importance of the history of the family. Unfamiliarity with the theoretical literature about the family as an institution has played a part in making them blind to the opportunities of analysis which their sources offer to them.'[29] He goes on to argue that 'there is a very close tie between the surge of interest in the history of the family and the parallel growth in historical demography. The connection is partly a matter of theoretical overlap and partly a result of dependence upon the same research techniques.'[30] Clearly, then, Wrigley recognizes the deficiencies of earlier population studies and emphasizes the importance of a sociological approach.

It will be useful to consider the distinctive features of the new methods and some of their implications. Traditional population history relied upon aggregative methods, upon totals of population present, upon the sum of children born or people dying. Its methods depended on two essential sources of data, the census (or its equivalent) and a source of vital registration. If either is lacking, as it usually is for any time before the mid-nineteenth century, the other could serve only a small number of purposes. The new methods involve family reconstitution using principally vital records, the basic methods being nominative rather than aggregative. Information about families is built up from sources, such as parish registers, in which individuals are named. All the records of birth, death and marriage relating to a particular family are brought together and consolidated into a single record. When this has been done the fertility and mortality of the reconstituted families can be investigated in great detail, and very intricate demographic analysis is possible.[31] Moreover, further information from other nominative sources can be used. Thus Poor Law records can be an additional source of data, and information about occupations obtained from marriage registers can be used to study social mobility. It is just by this sort of approach that Laslett[32] has shed much light on the part played by servants in pre-industrial England, Laslett having relied on information about variations in the size of households. In addition, as Wrigley suggests, these nominative studies enable studies of, say, age at marriage and economic opportunity to be investigated. Wrigley goes on to suggest the importance of this micro-analytic approach in, for example, examining variations in the age of marriage between different social groups, examining differences between urban and rural households, looking at social, economic and demographic characteristics of migrants. Most importantly, however, it is possible that this sort of study can contribute at a theoretical level to the problem of understanding the origins of industrialization in western Europe. In western Europe in the sixteenth, seventeenth and eighteenth centuries very few girls married before their late twenties. In addition there were large numbers of adolescent boys and girls in service. In England it is possible, therefore, that women passed in marriage only about half the period of their lives during which they were capable of bearing children. Equally, a substantial proportion of their active lives was spent without responsibilities for dependants. It could be argued that late marriage, by reducing fertility, may have helped to preserve a relatively favourable ratio of resources to population while at the same time producing a lifetime pattern of saving and expenditure more favourable to economic growth. Clearly such hypotheses are relevant not only to understanding industrialization in England in the eighteenth and nineteenth centuries, but also the problems of development in Asia and Africa today. The whole approach illustrates the interaction which might arise between historical research and sociological theory.

In a different area Professor and Dr Banks have shown how historical study and contemporary social investigation might come to bear upon the same problems and even, possibly, suggest policy recommendations. Thus Mr and Mrs Banks, after studying feminist movements and the decline in fertility in late nineteenth-century England, suggested that the decisions of the male in respect of birth control were the important ones.[33] An exactly similar conclusion was reached by Stylos[34] after his investigation of surveys conducted in post-war non-Western societies. The possible significance of these sets of findings for contemporary policy in respect of birth control campaigns should be obvious. Altogether it is easy to agree with Wrigley when he argues that working in this vein enables historians 'to have their cake and eat it'.[35] For what appears as essentially an idiographic discipline with its concern for the individual – at birth, marriage or death – translates easily into a nomothetic activity with an important contribution to make to understanding general rules and patterns found in societies. Thus 'this intricate and exhaustive enquiry into the minutiae of family life goes hand in hand with the opportunity to understand better the changes which separate our world from Shakespeare's and to do so in terms which further the understanding of social and economic change generally.'[36]

Another important field in which sociological methods have a contribution to make to historical study is in the explanation of major social movements of the past, as Professor Swanson has done in his work on the Reformation, which he actually subtitles *A Sociological Account of the Reformation*.[37] Swanson takes as his starting-point the work of Emile Durkheim on the functions of religion. His aim is to make this work more precise by conducting a substantive study. The whole activity, along with the critical attacks of the historians, can be used to illustrate the possibilities inherent in a sociological approach and the differences which can exist between historians and sociologists.

At the beginning of his book Swanson states his general argument: 'Beliefs in gods or other spirits,' he writes, 'arise as symbols of men's experience with the basic purpose and decision making procedures of societies and of enduring and independent groups within societies.'[38] Swanson attempts to confirm this explanatory generalization by examining the religious diversity apparent in sixteenth-century Europe, and showing that the general proposition accounts for why some European states remained Catholic whilst others turned to Protestantism; and also why Protestant states became, variously, Lutheran, Anglican or Calvinist. Thus, Swanson has begun from a theoretical position, from which he has developed hypotheses which he sets out to test against the historical data.

Swanson argues that man's conception of God is derived from his experience with government. In his view a theology commands general acceptance as long as it reflects the operation of political authority as this is felt to impinge upon human activity. Conversely, when theology loses this relation to political experience, pressures for religious change build up. Swanson says that this is precisely what happened in late medieval Europe, and that the new theologies of the sixteenth century functioned as necessary adaptations to changing political structures.

Catholicism, according to this perspective, reflected situations in which political regimes were experienced as 'immanent', that is, where a central governor did not share control over the regime, but exercised a direct authority over the whole society. Under such conditions, central authority permeated everywhere as an immediate experience. In this way it encouraged a most plausible and sacramental theology, which in parallel fashion conceived a spiritual power as potentially present and at work, that is 'immanent', in the world. Protestantism, by contrast, reflected those politics in which governing authority had come to seem remote or 'transcendent' through varying degrees of sharing. 'In some governments,' Swanson writes,[39]

> persons or groups participate in the regime not as its members or agents but as members of the society's political community and, when they do, the acts of the regime represent not an embodiment of the common interest but of relations between the regime and the several special interests now involved in its affairs. In such acts there cannot be said to be immanence because the structure and acts of government embody not the personal traits of a single collective actor but the interrelations among several actors ...

the theological analogue here being a transcendent God and a relatively anti-sacramental view of the world. Thus while Catholicism seems roughly equivalent to despotism, Protestantism emerges in some general relation to a corporatively organized society.

The greater part of Swanson's book is devoted to testing these general views by correlating the political structures of some forty-one European societies with their eventual theological preferences. As his theory had led him to predict, every 'centralist' regime (Austria, France, Jülich and Berg, Ireland, the Scottish Highlands, Portugal, Spain and the Swiss cantons of Lucerne and Solothurn) turn out to have remained Catholic. 'Limited centralist' regimes in which 'governors' formally shared power with local authorities who acted as their agents (Denmark, Sweden, England and some of the major German states) chose a moderate Protestantism in which a residual sacramentalism implied that God was not yet conceived as utterly transcendent. 'Balanced regimes', on the other hand, in which the governor formally shared with constituent bodies in the making of central policies (Bohemia, Hungary and Transylvania, the Scottish Lowlands, Geneva) adopted a fully transcendent theology and became Calvinist. Though there are two lesser categories in Swanson's classification, the major analysis should be clear.

Clearly then, Swanson's approach does provide a basis for historical inquiry of the kind likely to give rise to a cumulative body of knowledge, by means of which earlier propositions, or better sets of propositions, can be revised, extended, or rejected by later research. Altogether it represents a good illustration of the application of sociological theory and methods to a historical problem. To highlight its features and to show how the historian might disagree with it I will conclude by drawing upon a historian's criticisms of Swanson's work.[40]

> ... for the historian any satisfactory explanation for the confessional choices of the sixteenth and seventeenth centuries must be based, not on a general theory, but on the specific circumstances of the settlement in each separate case. The historian asks: who or what groups influenced the decision, for what motives, and under what conditions? And again, what special circumstances made the decision stick? ... From this standpoint, for example, Spain remained Catholic not because her government was 'experienced' in a peculiar way by Spanish society but because of a tradition of militant Catholicism associated with the mediaeval crusades, and because the reforms of Cardinal Ximenes reduced kinds of dissatisfaction that operated elsewhere. The Italian city states remained Catholic through a combination of proximity to Rome and political pressure. France stayed Catholic because this proved consistent, for special historical reasons, with a high degree of ecclesiastical autonomy, and permitted much the same diversity of religious sensibility, corresponding to the special needs of special groups, as was present in England.

So then, we have the sociologist and the historian.

Another important field in which sociological methods and techniques might be very relevant to the historian is in connection with the explanation of political and electoral history. Historical explanations in this area are usually of a highly rational kind; political man appears as just an extension of economic man. Shifts in voting patterns are discussed almost exclusively in terms of the public issues involved. Significant data are the speeches of political leaders, newspaper reports and editorial comments, and political and public campaigns. Yet such approaches must clearly be deemed inadequate in view of what political sociologists have now been able to tell us about, say, the voting patterns of the working-class electorate,[41] the importance of family and early socialization upon voting habits, the influence of public campaigns, the significance of status discrepancy amongst those who hold liberal opinions.[42] No wonder that Lenski[43] has complained that much of the failure of political history has been caused by the fact that many historians have attempted to explain political changes without doing the necessary research on easily available voting statistics.

In a similar way historians make generalizations about national character differences. Metzger has suggested[44] that attempts might be made to verify these through multivariate analysis. As he points out, one of the major problems in obtaining conclusions about national character is to distinguish among attributes of societies those which are properly characteristic of the culture and those which result from the fact that societies vary in their internal composition, containing more of certain social groups than another. Thus the question may arise as to whether society X differs from Y because it is predominantly rural, or Catholic, or has a much higher level of education, rather than because its basic values or 'character' vary. To test out these possibilities he suggests the use of a relatively straightforward sociological technique, namely, to hold factors constant as is done in intra-national opinion research. Thus one may compare English Jews with American Jews, or English graduates with Americans of comparable education.

In yet another area of political history the sociologist Sidney Aronson[45] has tested the various but frequent assumptions made by historians concerning the introduction of the spoils system by President Andrew Jackson in the United States of America. Aronson carefully coded the social background characteristics of the higher civil servants in the administrations of John Adams, Thomas

Jefferson, and of John Quincy Adams and Andrew Jackson, much as might be done with interview data. As a result he is able to show that the overwhelming majority in all four administrations came from the socio–economic élite. The study illustrates the way in which contemporary observers may be deceived about what is happening around them, particularly when they are making guesses about facts which are actually unavailable to them, and more especially when the issue under consideration might be the subject of political debate. Thus Andrew Jackson sought to appeal to a mass electorate and may have hoped to have gained more advantage in claiming that he was replacing the old Federalists with straightforward men of the people, Democrats. His friends and his enemies may well have accepted what appeared to be his action, and thus have misled not only contemporaries but also future historians.

An important source of data often neglected by historians is the opinion survey. Over the last thirty years commercial and academic polling organizations have accumulated a great variety of data about such things as the state of public opinion, church attendance, voting behaviours and membership of voluntary organizations. In the future such data will be vital to historians as much of their work involves making assumptions about the state of public opinion and changes in it. Paul Lazarsfeld who has done much to initiate and develop surveys of attitudes and opinions has pointed out the need for a reappraisal of historical writing in the light of the argument that the development of opinion surveys has changed the notion of a 'fact'. He has pointed out that at one time only political documents of an archive kind were considered appropriate evidence for the historian. This consideration made him focus on political events – everything else was interpretation. Then the 'new history' in the United States centred attention on data such as economic and social statistics, and this enlarged considerably the area of what were considered facts. 'Still,' writes Lazarsfeld, 'sentiments and attitudes remained a matter of interpretation. Now, however, they too have become facts. The result of a public opinion poll is as much a fact as the content of a political document or the crop and price statistics of a certain region.'[46]

Lazarsfeld also points out two major deficiencies of this kind of work which are particularly relevant to historians. Firstly, the problem of saliency. The fact that a respondent answers a question put to him still does not tell us whether he would have asked himself this question or whether the matter is of particular concern to him. Secondly, the diffusion of opinion in time and social space is a problem which is not yet handled with enough emphasis or enough technical skill. Far more knowledge is required both from a sociological and historical perspective about the sources of people's ideas and how they pass them on. Thus in another work I have asserted that between 1918 and 1944

> Technological progress, changes in the occupational structure and two world wars all helped to identify problems and change values and beliefs associated with the educational system. Finally it was becoming clear that arguments in terms of economic efficiency, individual opportunity and social justice were counting for more and more.[47]

Obviously, it is very difficult to test the validity of such statements, yet their verification is of great importance to historians in understanding how attitudes change over time. Moreover, as the quotation indicates, it is essential to comprehend the relationship between changes in the structural features of a society and changes in the beliefs, values and ideologies held by members of that society. It might be reasonable to suppose that future historians will have available, and will be prepared to use, data from opinion pollsters which would help to provide the important answers.

In concluding this discussion of some of the sociological techniques and methods which might be used in historical study I will return both to education and to a classic sociological approach – that of the comparative method. An appropriate illustration is, of course, Lawrence Stone's paper 'Education and Modernization in Japan and England'.[48] Stone compares the social structure, educational programme and economic growth of Japan with those of England from the mid-sixteenth century to the early twentieth century. The comparative method is basic to the social sciences. Emile Durkheim has described it as the primary instrument of social research and Comte used to refer to the 'comparative *or* historical method'. The benefits to be achieved by this method are numerous. By classifying the resemblances and differences displayed by phenomena deemed to be comparable, causal factors in the emergence and development of such phenomena and patterns of inter-relation both within and between such phenomena might be classified and elicited. Such an approach, following upon Stone's work, has obvious relevance to

understanding the part played by educational systems in con-
tributing to economic growth in different societies, and in the same
society over time.[49]

Finally, we might consider the implications of the techniques and
methods that I have discussed for the study of the history of education. It is possible to suggest that too much of the history of education is of a purely formal kind. The focus is upon legislation;
government and administrative policy; growth in the number of
pupils, teachers, schools; changing relationships between central and
local government, the changing basis of financial support: yet there
remain areas, scrutiny of which is vital to our understanding of the
position of the educational system in relation to the total society. I
have already suggested the possible value of historical perspectives
on the relationship between education and economic growth; but
those aspects of the history of education concerning social structures
and processes of change are rarely investigated in an explicit fashion
by those who study education. Consequently there is an almost complete lack of historical work in connection with social change and
social mobility, of the part played by education in modernization, or
of its function in relation to changing and modifying values.

On the other hand, thinking more positively about future research
one can reflect on the possibilities for the history of education. The
simple classification suggested by Turner[50] of 'sponsored' and
'contest' systems of mobility in connection with educational systems
could be developed further. Perhaps even greater potential exists
within the far wider-ranging typology proposed by Earl Hopper.[51]
Indeed, one is tempted to suggest that there is room for a study of
educational systems which has the scope of Swanson's analysis of the
Reformation. More fruitful, perhaps, might be to consider change in
the educational system in relation to change in the total society as
Basil Bernstein has argued[52] should be done, utilizing the concepts
of 'mechanical' and 'organic' solidarity to focus attention on changes
in a number of vital areas: structure of education, the curricula, the
pedagogy, the roles of the teacher, the personal qualities of the pupils
and educational ideologies. Perhaps it is not too much to hope that
those who work in the field of education, with its wide-ranging perspectives and tradition of inter-disciplinary activity, might pioneer
historical sociology in order that we might better understand not
only the educational system, but also the educational process.

Notes

1 G. C. Homans, *The Human Group* (London: Routledge and Kegan Paul, 1951), p. 22.
2 A. V. Cicourel, *The Social Organization of Juvenile Justice* (New York: Wiley, 1968), pp. 10–11.
3 C. W. Mills, *The Sociological Imagination* (New York: Oxford University Press, 1959), p. 143.
4 Ibid., p. 145.
5 J. H. Plumb, 'The Historian's Dilemma', in J. H. Plumb (ed.), *Crisis in the Humanities* (Harmondsworth: Pelican, 1964), p. 28.
6 Ibid., p. 30.
7 L. Stone, 'Literacy and Education in England 1640–1900', *Past and Present*, No. 42 (February 1969), p. 69.
8 S. W. F. Holloway, 'What History is and What it Ought to be', in W. H. Burston and D. Thompson (eds.), *Studies in the Nature and Teaching of History* (London: Routledge and Kegan Paul, 1967), p. 13.
9 A. Ryan, *Philosophy of the Social Sciences* (London: Macmillan, 1970), p. 181.
10 T. B. Bottomore, *Introduction to Sociology* (London: Allen and Unwin, 1962), p. 25.
11 R. K. Merton, *Social Theory and Social Structure* (Chicago: Free Press, 1957), p. 16.
12 Ibid., p. 100.
13 W. H. Walsh, *Introduction to the Philosophy of History* (London: Hutchinson, 1951), p. 41.
14 S. Hook, 'Problems of Terminology in Historical Writing – Illustrations', *Theory and Practice in Historical Study*, S.S.R.C. Bulletin No. 54 (New York, 1946), as quoted in S. W. F. Holloway, op. cit., p. 4.
15 S. W. F. Holloway, op. cit., pp. 4–10.
16 Ibid., p. 5.
17 See W. O. Aydelotte, 'Notes on the Problem of Historical Generalization', in L. Gottschalk (ed.), *Generalization in the Writing of History* (University of Chicago Press, 1963), pp. 145–77.
18 W. I. Thomas and F. Znaniecki, *The Polish Peasant in Europe and America* (New York: Dover Publications, 1927), p. 37.
19 J. A. Banks, 'Historical Sociology and the Study of Population', *Daedalus* (Spring 1968), p. 398.
20 H. S. Hughes, 'The Historian and the Social Scientist', *American Historical Review*, Vol. LXVI (1960), pp. 20–46.
21 E. A. Wrigley, 'Population, Family and Household', in M. Ballard (ed.), *New Movements in the Study and Teaching of History* (London: Temple-Smith, 1970), p. 95. I have drawn heavily on this concise article.
22 G. Rudé, *The Crowd in the French Revolution* (Oxford: Clarendon Press, 1959).

23 J. R. Vincent, *Pollbooks: How Victorians Voted* (Cambridge University Press, 1967).
24 R. Hofstadter, 'History and Sociology in the United States', in S. M. Lipset and R. Hofstadter (eds.), *Sociology and History: Methods* (New York: Basic Books, 1968), p. 15.
25 L. Gottschalk, C. Kluckhohn and R. Angell, *The Use of Personal Documents in History, Anthropology and Sociology*, S.S.R.C. Bulletin No. 53 (New York, 1945).
26 C. V. Langois and C. Seignobos, *Introduction to the Study of History* (London: Duckworth, 1906), p. 67.
27 G. Bernbaum, *The Role of the Headmaster*, a research study supported by the Social Science Research Council (1972).
28 H. D. Lasswell, N. Leites *et al.*, *Language of Politics* (New York: M.I.T. Press, 1949).
29 E. A. Wrigley, op. cit., p. 93.
30 Ibid., p. 94.
31 See E. A. Wrigley (ed.), *An Introduction to English Historical Demography* (London: Weidenfeld and Nicolson, 1966).
32 P. Laslett, *The World We Have Lost* (London: Methuen, 1965).
33 J. A. and O. Banks, *Prosperity and Parenthood* (London: Routledge and Kegan Paul, 1954).
34. J. M. Stylos, 'The Outlook for World Population', *Science* (11 December 1964), p. 1438.
35 E. A. Wrigley, 'Population, Family and Household', p. 102.
36 Ibid.
37 G. E. Swanson, *Religion and Regime: A Sociological Account of the Reformation* (Ann Arbor: University of Michigan Press, 1967).
38 Ibid., Preface.
39 Ibid., p. 39.
40 See W. J. Bouwsma, 'Swanson's Reformation', *Comparative Studies in Society and History*, Vol. X (1967–8), pp. 486–91.
41 E. A. Nordlinger, *The Working Class Tories* (London: Macgibbon and Kee, 1967).
42 R. T. Mackenzie and A. Silver, *Angels in Marble: Working Class Conservatism in Urban England* (London: Heinemann, 1968).
43 G. E. Lenski, *Power and Privilege: A Theory of Social Stratification* (New York: McGraw-Hill, 1966).
44 W. Metzger, 'Generalizations about National Character: An Analytical Essay', in L. Gottschalk (ed.), *Generalization in the Writing of History* (University of Chicago Press, 1963), pp. 90–4.
45 S. Aronson, *Status and Kinship in the Higher Civil Service* (Cambridge, Mass.: Harvard University Press, 1964).
46 P. F. Lazarsfeld, 'The Historian and the Pollster', in S. M. Lipset and R. Hofstadter (eds.), op. cit., p. 393.
47 G. Bernbaum, *Social Change and the Schools 1918–44* (London: Routledge and Kegan Paul, 1967), p. 115.
48 See *Comparative Studies in Society and History*, Vol. IX (1966–7), pp. 208–32.

49 G. E. Hurd and T. J. Johnson, 'Education and Development', *Sociological Review*, Vol. 15 (1967).
50 R. H. Turner, 'Modes of Social Ascent through Education; Sponsored and Contest Mobility', in A. H. Halsey, J. Floud and C. A. Anderson (eds.), *Education, Economy and Society* (New York: Free Press, 1961).
51 E. I. Hopper, 'A Typology for the Classification of Educational Systems', *Sociology*, Vol. 2, No. 1 (1968).
52 B. Bernstein, 'Open Schools; Open Society', *New Society* (14 September 1967).

R. K. KELSALL

Intellectual merit and higher civil service recruitment: the rise and fall of an idea

This paper concerns the rise and fall of an idea, a rise and fall that has spanned a century. The idea I am concerned with was, in essence, that an intellectual élite of young people should be selected annually, by an open competition testing only their *intellectual* capacity by written examinations of a rigorous and demanding type, to fill junior but responsible posts in the British Home Civil Service. And that the holders of the highest offices in that Service would subsequently be chosen mainly from those who had entered in this way. The germ of this idea, as everyone knows, was contained in the *Report on the Organization of the Permanent Civil Service* submitted to Gladstone by Sir Stafford Northcote and Sir Charles Trevelyan in November 1853. They proposed that two categories of post should be distinguished, 'intellectual and mechanical'; that patronage should be replaced by recruitment through open competitive examinations for both types of post; and that promotion should in future not be by seniority but by merit. As a result of the storm of controversy that inevitably ensued, there was considerable delay before proposals of such a revolutionary kind could be generally applied. Progress, though slow, did nevertheless take place. In 1855 a Civil Service Commission was established to take over from individual departments the conduct of such examinations and personal enquiries about candidates as were called for. And from the same year Writerships in the Indian Civil Service were filled by open competitive examinations. Oxford and Cambridge increasingly introduced systematic examinations for degree and other purposes. And, when the franchise was extended in 1867, political patronage became ineffective.

By 1870 the way was, therefore, clear for the next step, Gladstone's Order in Council of 4 June. This directed that all vacancies of certain types should in future be filled by open competition; and subsequent Treasury regulations provided a detailed framework for

c

this to be done, including open examinations for men of university standard to fill the higher posts. It is, therefore, particularly appropriate that in 1970, a hundred years later, we should be celebrating the centenary of that Order in Council by discussing the subsequent history of the revolutionary idea contained within it.

We must, of course, be very careful not to distort history by reading too much into what was taking place. There was no intention, and no possibility even had there been such an intention, of giving access to these key posts to social strata below those which monopolized the great public schools and universities. Even bearing this limitation in mind, however, a great deal was achieved as, in the years that followed 1870, one department after another adopted the new procedures. A disparate collection of important public service posts became a profession, access to which was open to any young man of the appropriate age who chose to submit himself to very high-standard testing of his intellectual abilities and knowledge in fields of his own choosing, and whose rank order on the results of these tests was high enough, given the number of vacancies to be filled.

Of course, these open competitive examinations had their teething troubles. To begin with, candidates could not only choose from a range of subjects, but could also elect to be examined in as few or as many of them as they liked. This sometimes gave an advantage to young men with a superficial knowledge of a number of subjects rather than a profound knowledge of a few. So the rules were altered in various ways to defeat the 'mere smatterer'. Too *narrow* a range might, however, be equally unsatisfactory, such as over-specialization in mathematics and science to the exclusion of history, philosophy or even English. So the marking scheme was modified in such a way as to penalize this also. By the time the MacDonnell Commission was sitting, on the eve of the outbreak of the First World War, it was being said that the Oxford man who took Classical Moderations followed by Greats had an advantage over those from other universities (including Cambridge) in that he alone could make up the necessary total of examination choices without going beyond his university subjects. There were also incidental costs (a month in London taking the examination, preceded by several months, and the necessary fees, at Wren's or some other London crammer) which often effectively precluded the poor man's son from competing with any chance of success. Whatever the reasons, four-fifths of those entering by the open competition route came from Oxford or Cambridge; though no one, in those pre-First World War days, expected this proportion to continue in the future, far less to be exceeded.

How far, by this time, had open competition become the *sole* route of entry to high administrative office in the Home Civil Service? It was certainly by far the most important route, but there were a few others. First of all, a very small number of departments managed to avoid falling into line, and filled their administrative vacancies by direct entrants chosen in other ways. The most notorious case, and I use the word deliberately, was that of the Board of Education. In that department, junior administrators were conveniently called Assistant Examiners, and their posts were accordingly held to be of a technical or specialist type which it was legitimate to fill on what was, to all intents and purposes, a patronage basis. Once the nature and extent of this loophole was brought fully to light by the MacDonnell Commission there could, however, be no question of its indefinite continuance. And from 1919 onwards this particular anomaly was eliminated.

A more defensible alternative route to open competition was promotion from the ranks. Whether or not those responsible for suggesting and introducing open competition had originally intended to create a complete social and educational cleavage within the service, in which there should be virtually no possibility of surmounting the internal barrier, official practice and pronouncements as the years went by seemed to be creating just such a situation. This was clearly how it looked to the 1,500 clerks in the Lower Division who in 1883 sent a Memorial to the Treasury by way of the Colonial Office asking, in effect, what their chances of crossing the bar might be if their merits seemed to justify promotion. The Treasury reply, though belated, was surprisingly conciliatory. Such promotees should not necessarily form an insignificant proportion of the Higher Division, and promotion across this boundary line could fairly be considered as a legitimate aspiration for superior Lower Division members. Moreover, a laborious piecing-together of what little information can be assembled suggests that, in the period preceding the 1914–18 war, something not far short of a fifth of the intake into the Higher Division tended to be in the form of the upgrading of exceptional Lower Division men, some of whom had originally entered as Boy Copyists or even Boy Messengers.

Direct entry on a patronage basis, promotion from the ranks and a very limited amount of transfer from specialist branches only accounted between them, however, for a small proportion of the upper echelons of the administrative hierarchy. Most of those who reached these heights, whether the foothills or the peaks, had been initially selected by an open competition intended to measure purely intellectual ability, with no necessary specific relevance to the tasks that would subsequently fall to their lot. The basic assumption was, of course, that those who showed themselves to be exceptionally able intellectually in their early twenties, regardless of the fields in which they did so, would in their thirties, forties and fifties be likely, by and large, to cope more successfully with the problems facing high-level administrators in the public service than would others selected on different criteria. And, despite the partly unavoidable handicaps to which the poor man's son was subject in such a competition, every effort was made to ensure that the open race for junior vacancies in the service was a fair one. The pursuit of the goal of efficiency was, in the main, compatible with the simultaneous pursuit of equality of access to public office amongst those of similar intellectual potential. And, with the increasing democratization of our society's educational arrangements, one could look forward in the not-too-distant future to a very close approach indeed to a higher civil service open to talents.

It was clear from the evidence given to the MacDonnell Commission that there was no serious dissatisfaction, inside or outside the service, either with the principle of an intellectually rigorous open competition or with its practical implementation. Some tidying-up might perhaps seem desirable, first to put on a more equal footing candidates in the main schools of study at *all* British universities, and secondly to ensure a reasonable standard of written English, ability to translate from a foreign language, and some conversance with contemporary problems social, economic and political as well as with the general principles, methods and applications of science. This tidying-up (mainly by way of a new, compulsory section of the competition) had to wait until the 1914–18 war was over, but was duly recommended by the Leathes Committee and put into operation after 1921. At the same time the major, but by then largely non-controversial, step was taken of throwing the competition open to women as well as men.

Open competitions had, of course, been suspended during the First World War, and in the special reconstruction competitions in the three following years, 1919, 1920 and 1921, a selection board interviewed those applicants who had survived a simple examination and other preliminaries. There was ample warrant for such a break with established procedure, if only because of the disruption of their education suffered by virtually all the candidates. When the normal open competitions were subsequently resumed (abortively in 1921 and effectively in 1925), however, the revolutionary step was taken of including an interview there as well. This formed such a major departure from the basic principle of recruitment purely on the basis of intellectual ability that some account must be given of how such a step came to be taken.

The MacDonnell Commission had, it is true, explored the possibility of introducing a viva, but had in the end made no such recommendation. Very few of those in the service who gave evidence were in favour of a change of this kind. Two did, however, support the idea. Mr Leathes, the First Civil Service Commissioner at that time, advocated, in his later evidence, a viva on some subject of the candidate's own choosing, the examiners being able to question him on matters of common knowledge as well. And Mr Mair, his Director of Examinations, talked of the importance of features not testable by written examinations – bearing and manners, whether one was a man of the world or merely a scholar. These two subsequently turned up as Chairman and Secretary respectively of the post-war Treasury Committee charged with tidying-up syllabus arrangements; and their committee additionally recommended the introduction of an interview as an integral part of the open competition.

Not only was the opinion of pre-war senior civil servants almost unanimously against such a change; witnesses from outside the service were also, in the main, opposed to it. D. J. Medley, Professor of History at Glasgow University, for example, pointed to the probable unfairness resulting when candidates with a very different social background from the members of the interviewing board were being assessed. 'Our men,' he said, 'are not English public school boys . . . they are quite a different type and they have not had the same opportunities; they have not the same outward polish and outside manner.' These prophetic words must have echoed in the ears of many a brilliant but tongue-tied candidate in the interview room at Burlington Gardens as his hopes of establishing a commanding lead in the competition on account of his marks for the *written* part of the examination were steadily whittled down and ultimately eliminated altogether as he realized the poor interview marks he would get as the fifteen-minute ordeal progressed.

There was no mandate for this revolutionary change, then, either from inside or outside the service. And any support for such an idea in educational circles related to a very different kind of viva from the one actually introduced, the viva to make sure that the candidate's intellectual grasp was really as impressive as his written work would suggest. No thought seems to have been given to any aspect of the matter. What, for instance, would be the appropriate weight to give this new component? Originally, 300 marks out of a total of 1800 was decided on; and then, as a by-product of some other changes in 1937, it became 300 out of 1,300. What qualities was it intended to test? The wording first used might sound relatively innocuous – alertness, intelligence and intellectual outlook, presence of mind and nervous equipoise – but how could one be sure, in a completely unstructured interview situation, that these, and not the social graces of the candidate, or the experiences he was fortunate enough to have had (abroad, for example), would prove to be what made the difference between a mark of 300 and a damning mark of 150 or even 50?

Such doubts did not, unfortunately, worry the Leathes Committee. Nor did they worry the First Commissioners who succeeded Sir Stanley and who filled the all-important role of chairmen of the interview boards. Indeed, Mr Meiklejohn had such faith in the procedure that he would have liked to make it a preliminary interview to weed out unsuitable candidates from proceeding to the written examination at all. Though this proposal was not in the end accepted, the Tomlin Commission, impressed by what seemed to them the success and smooth working of the interview arrangement, made no suggestion for change. Yet evidence was accumulating that interviews might not be such a good idea as those who conducted them believed them to be. At an international conference on examinations held at Folkestone in 1935 (following one at Eastbourne in 1931), for example, it was shown that pairs of interviews of exactly the type used for the administrative class competitions gave such different marks as almost to mask the common influence that they were dealing with the same set of candidates. Everything seemed to turn on the chance of the board's hitting on a topic which gave the particular candidate being interviewed the opportunity he needed to show himself in the most favourable light.

What worried many of us about these interviews in the period between the wars was not just their unpredictability and unreliability, serious though these defects undoubtedly were. It was, of course, that such a procedure might eliminate altogether from the race candidates who were intellectually better than, but socially inferior to, their fellow competitors. And it is to this aspect of the matter that I now wish to turn. Needless to say, all concerned with the interviewing hotly denied either that this was their intention, *or* that this could possibly be the result (even the unintended result) of their actions. And convincing evidence on this latter point was altogether lacking.

It seemed clear to me that something ought to be done to fill this gap. A first approach to throwing light on what was happening lay in assembling and analysing the published data on marks awarded for the two main components of the open competition on the one hand and the last schools attended by the candidates concerned on the other. For those who had entered by this route in the six years before the First World War (when the examination was entirely a written one), there proved to be no statistically significant difference between the average mark of men who had been at Clarendon Commission schools (that is, Eton, Winchester, Westminster, Charterhouse, St Paul's, Merchant Taylors', Harrow, Rugby and Shrewsbury) and men who had not. Nor was there any difference in the average marks of men who had been at predominantly boarding schools and those whose schools had been mainly catering for day pupils. When we look at the successful candidates in the inter-war open competitions of 1925 to 1939, however, the position was very different. To begin with, in the written part of the assessment, those from day schools did better than those from boarding ones; those from non-Clarendon schools did better than those from the nine Clarendon schools; and the 95 entrants from local education authority schools had average marks significantly higher than those of their 389 counterparts from independent and direct grant schools.

In the case of the inter-war open competition entrants we can do the same exercise for their interview marks. When this is done, we find the position completely reversed. In what was for them obviously the highly favourable climate of a fifteen or twenty-minute dialogue with board members of similar social and educational background to themselves, the entrants from Clarendon schools scored significantly higher marks than those from the schools attended by the remainder of the entrants, which was something that neither their pre-war predecessors nor they themselves had been able to do in the anonymous, written part of the examination. Similarly, those from boarding schools did better at the interview than those from day schools. And the 95 from local education authority schools fared significantly worse than those from independent and direct grant schools, in striking contrast to their superiority in the written examinations.

A second line of approach is to consider how successfully the marks awarded predicted the speed of subsequent promotion of these open competition entrants. Here it is sufficient to say that the marks for both parts of the competition were positively correlated with rapidity of later promotion, but that the correlation was significantly greater when the marks for written work were being compared with career success than when those for the interview were involved.

A third approach entailed a detailed analysis of unpublished data relating to *unsuccessful* candidates as well as published material for successful ones. The Civil Service Commission would only give permission for this to be done for a single year, 1938. The results were, however, startling. If we shorten the account by moving direct to its final stage, we find that, of 76 candidates who qualified for the offer of a post, 18 would not have done so but for the *improvement* in their overall order-of-merit brought about by very good interview marks. Had the competition been on pre-war lines, they would have been replaced by another group of 18 who, but for the *deterioration* in their overall order-of-merit brought about by less good interview marks, would have been eligible for the offer of a post. A turnover of this magnitude, nearly 24 per cent, clearly showed that the interview was doing much more than merely weeding out a few candidates who would have been, in the Board's opinion, unsuitable.

When the two groups of 18 were compared with each other they proved to be very different in their educational and social background. Of those who owed their offer of a post to the interview, 13 had fathers in the Registrar General's two top social class categories, as compared with only 7 of those in the displaced group, and this difference was statistically significant. The same kind of tendency was seen to be at work when the schools and universities of the two groups were compared.

These three lines of approach, then, provide strong evidence to support the view that, however good the intentions of board members, an interview on the inter-war model inevitably favours those with certain types of family origin and educational experience. It is, of course, arguable that, both in their own interests and in those of the service, those who are not completely successful in such an interview situation ought to be rejected. This argument is plausible when one is considering the weeding-out of the obviously unfit. At the margin where interview marks become crucial, however, there is no evidence that, for instance, the public interest was better served by offering posts (in the 1938 example) to 18 people with poorer marks in the written part of the examination rather than another 18 who were assessed as being intellectually superior but whose interviews did not come off as well. And, as we have seen, in terms of predicting career success in the service, marks for the written part of the examination have the edge over marks for the viva. In these circumstances, the public interest is surely best served by an open competition which is perceived by prospective candidates to be as free of social bias as it can be. That the inter-war competitions were not felt to match up to this requirement is shown by the extent to which Oxford and Cambridge candidates continued to preponderate, and even to increase their preponderance, thus falsifying Viscount Haldane's 1912 prediction when he said 'I should be seriously disappointed if, in twenty-five years, the new universities do not send up a proportion of candidates very nearly approaching Oxford and Cambridge.'

The introduction of a viva as an integral part of the open competition in the 1920s represented, then, the first major breach (and, to many observers, an entirely unwarranted one) in the idea of selection on intellectual merit alone. The second major breach came, of course, with the decision after the Second World War that up to a quarter (and later up to a half) of those recruited to the administrative class by open competition should compete by Method II. There were many attractive features about the new procedure. It paid some regard specifically to the work those recruited would afterwards have to do, by tests both on an individual and on a group basis which presented candidates with a range of appropriate concrete situations. The whole process could be regarded as an extended interview of a highly structured kind, in which the chance elements of the inter-war short general interview no longer dominated the situation. Unlike the traditional written examinations of Method I, long and arduous preparation was not required, and candidates who chose Method II were saved the work and worry of what amounted, in effect, to two sets of finals papers in close proximity to each other. Even before the Fulton Committee recommended the complete replacement of the old method by the new (with suitable amendments) it was obvious that, once an alternative was available, the unpopularity of written examinations of this rigorous and demanding type would sound their death knell. Moreover, from the point of view of the candidate of humble social origin, the anonymity of a written examination in which he was only known by a number had already ceased to be of any avail when, in the 1920s, he was required to present himself for interview.

Spurned alike by candidates and by the architects of recruitment plans, the idea, which it was the purpose of this paper to consider, has clearly outlived its usefulness. At its best, it probably combined as well as any recruitment policy could have done at the time the interests of the efficiency of the service on the one hand, and social justice to talented young citizens on the other. At its worst, in the inter-war years, it represented an uneasy compromise between the Civil Service Commission's simultaneous pursuit of the intellectually able and the socially acceptable. Let us hope that the new principles and policies of the 1970s will meet our society's needs as well as did those of the 1870s.

Note

An indication of sources, and more detailed supporting evidence for most of the statements made and opinions expressed in this paper, will be found in the author's study *Higher Civil Servants in Britain* (London: Routledge and Kegan Paul, 1955; reprinted 1966).

FRANK MUSGROVE

Historical materials for the study of the bureaucratization of education

I am interested in the bureaucratization of the contemporary school. It therefore seems relevant to ask questions about power and authority in Victorian schools. These questions seem to me to be relevant for two reasons: first, because I see history as a normative study. It is normative because it is comparative. I wish to make value-judgements about educational bureaucracy today, and I can do this principally on the basis of comparison. Second, I wish to test a variety of hypotheses about the operation and consequences of bureaucracy; and the hypotheses should find support, or refutation, in historical no less than in contemporary data. I have no interest in history for its own sake, and cannot readily conceive what this can mean. My difficulty is that historians have not been asking questions about Victorian schools, and the school system, which would produce the information I need for my twin purposes.

Both E. H. Carr and J. H. Plumb advocate history which is comparative-normative; and Peter Laslett actually writes it. Carr would use history to make moral judgements about institutions, but not about individuals. The historian cannot pass judgement on an individual oriental despot: he is a creature of his age; but the historian's comparative studies enable him to pass judgement on oriental despotism in comparison with the institutions of Periclean Athens.[1] Plumb appears to have a similar conception of history when he makes a plea for the reinstatement of the idea of progress at the centre of historical studies: 'to ignore the implication of the concept of progress seems to me to lead to disintegration, nihilism, and to the proliferation of meaningless investigations. In so doing historians turn their back on their social function' (and their students, at least at Cambridge, learn to treat history as 'an intellectual pastime, with little rhyme and less reason'[2]).

Careful (and preferably quantitative) historical study may show that the rise of bureaucracy, like the decline of the family, has been a non-event: and our judgement of contemporary bureaucracy will be correspondingly changed. Crozier is already suggesting, on rather slight, impressionistic evidence, that the broad European trend since the sixteenth century has been toward less bureaucracy – or less bureaucratic bureaucracy – rather than more.[3] (But bureaucracy is complex and many-sided, and all its sides have certainly not changed in unison.) We need more precise indicators, like some that have been used in studies of the family. When I first looked at the statistics of the N.S.P.C.C. I confidently expected to find a rising number of cases of ill-treatment and neglect. The unanimous verdict at that time (some seven or eight years ago) was that the family was in decline; latch-key children were a byword in every school common-room; and surely this would be reflected in the records of the N.S.P.C.C.

In fact I found an improvement so remarkable and so rapid that it qualifies, I think, for the label 'revolution'. In 1900 there had been over 3,000 prosecutions for ill-treatment and neglect; in 1964, 400. This decrease has been fairly steady over 60 years; the much smaller number occurred in a population which was bigger by a third; and the criteria of neglect had certainly not been relaxed.[4] My perception and judgement of the contemporary family was profoundly influenced by the demonstration of this historical trend. But, of course, the family, like bureaucracy, has many sides; and divorce statistics tell a different story – though by no means especially disquieting when set alongside the statistics of longevity.

Peter Laslett has made much more elaborate and sophisticated comparative studies and has been able to quantify the amount of aid given within pre-industrial, compared with contemporary, families. And his comparative study is inevitably a moral study, an examination of progress, just as Plumb would wish. Thus, for instance, after all due allowances have been made, Laslett shows that the pre-industrial middle-aged couple was far less willing than today to provide a place in their home for elderly relatives.[5] Even Michael Young's Woodford begins to take on a slightly different complexion.

A common indicator of bureaucratization is the changing ratio of support to front-line personnel. Bendix has calculated that in the first half of the twentieth century the ratio of administrative to production employees in British industry rose from approximately 8 to 20 per cent.[6] It should not be a difficult exercise to compute this ratio for different points in time, since the later nineteenth century, for English education. An important distinction might be made between in-school and system-wide bureaucratization. My guess is that according to this measure the schools themselves have been steadily debu-reaucratized, surviving with a diminishing proportion of administrative personnel (it is astonishing what a headmaster with a secretary and a clerk-typist is still able to do); and that even a system-wide calculation would show less bureaucratization than in-dustry. Independent schools and direct-grant schools survive with-out the service of external (or displaced) bureaucracy, and with only a skeletal bureaucracy within. Of course teachers may become part-time bureaucrats – and so indeed may pupils, as attendance moni-tors, milk monitors and the like. Pupils are a reservoir of part-time bureaucrats on the cheap – as Arnold was perhaps the first to realize. But when all due allowances have been made, I suspect that schools are under-bureaucratized – compared with factories, armies and hos-pitals. The crisis over 'auxiliaries' is a symptom of this condition.

Historical data in this area will not only shift our perspectives and our judgements; they will also provide the means to test important hypotheses. I suspect that the alleged relationship between bureau-cratization and organizational size will not show up on this par-ticular indicator; but the less familiar hypothesis, that democracy and bureaucracy are closely related, will. Bureaucracy follows closely in the wake of internal self-government and all schemes of 'participation'. The history of the universities shows this most clearly (and dramatically in the case of the C.A.T.s, where the registry, rather than the output of technologists, has been the major growth point since they became universities, with all the familiar apparatus of senates and committees). Democracy means keeping records, transmitting decisions, preparing agenda and supporting papers, minutes and reports. In school pupil-parliaments have been well served by pupil-bureaucrats; and one urgent study is not the bureau-cratization of the teacher, but of the pupil role. (Members of the first sixth form that I ever taught, in a boarding school, were endlessly writing out lists when I thought they were carefully noting my re-interpretation of Bismarck.)

Bureaucracy is a misleadingly simple notion, and, if the historian is to help the sociologist, he must be told what it means and what indicators might be serviceable. Max Weber's writings on the subject are already overlaid with a heavy commentary, and the relation-ships he saw between various features of organizational life have been put to some empirical test. A simple, unitary concept of bureaucracy is no longer tenable.

Bureaucracies co-ordinate the diverse activities of specialists and organize them in a rational plan. They enjoin discipline and predictable behaviour. Max Weber described the 'ideal-type' bureaucracy. Its essential characteristics are five in number: there is a clear-cut division of labour, and regular activities 'are distributed in a fixed way as official duties'; the organization is hierarchical, 'each lower office is under the control and supervision of a higher one'; there is a system of rules, and operations are governed by 'the application of these rules to particular cases'; the conduct of officials is impersonal, and duties are performed 'without hatred or passion, and hence without affection or enthusiasm'; and employment is based on technical qualifications, it is protected against arbitrary dismissal, and it 'constitutes a career. There is a system of promotions according to seniority or to achievement, or both.'[7]

Max Weber's account of bureaucratic organization has received close critical scrutiny and has been put to some empirical test. The original 'dimensions' of bureaucracy have been refined and elaborated. But most important of all are the clear indications in recent research that the various aspects of bureaucracy are relatively independent: organizations may, for example, have a well-defined system of rules without being particularly hierarchical, or may emphasize technical competence without placing stress on either specialization or impersonality of official conduct. A study of ten American organizations showed that there was very little correlation among the various classical dimensions of bureaucracy.[8] An elaborate factor-analytical study by Pugh and Hickson based on observations in fifty-two English work organizations led to a similar conclusion and suggestions for renaming the four major dimensions that seemed to emerge. Pugh and Hickson claim: 'As a result of this dimensional analysis, it is clear that to talk in terms of the bureaucratic ideal type is not adequate, since the structure of an organization may vary along any of these four empirical dimensions.'[9]

This research into contemporary organizations is important not least because it enables us to look realistically at bureaucratization as a historical development. We need not expect to find all aspects of bureaucracy changing together and in unison. Thus we do not necessarily expect that a more hierarchical organization of education automatically goes hand-in-hand with greater centralization. Indeed, a close examination of changes in the organization of the education service in general and of schools in particular over the past hundred years shows these bureaucratic features in complete disarray: while some march forward steadily, others retreat. The most steady advance since the later nineteenth century probably relates to the employment of teachers on the basis of technical qualifications, protected against arbitrary dismissal, and constituting a career. Centralization, on the other hand, shows a more complicated pattern of advance and retreat. (It is curious that very little work seems to have been done on centralization since George Baron published his important paper on the headmaster 14 years ago.[10])

There is abundant material on schools and universities in the nineteenth century – in the form of school records, and the reports of Government commissions – which would reveal the nature of these trends if we addressed the right questions to it. It would provide, for example, job-descriptions: what, precisely, could headmasters and their assistants take decisions about; who could constrain whom and for what purposes; who could hire and fire, and on what grounds; who was superior or inferior to whom, and in what did this superiority or inferiority consist? I have searched standard histories and the histories of particular schools, and find it very difficult to find answers to these apparently straightforward questions. The Clarendon and Taunton Commissions are more helpful; and among contemporary historians of education, Bamford is especially useful.[11] But I have found it difficult to discover the duties and terms of service of tutors and fellows at Oxford colleges. V. H. H. Green's recent book, *The Universities* (1969), for example, is singularly unhelpful.

The opposite of bureaucratic employment is fee-paid service to clients. The loyalties are different: in the former case it is to the organization, in the latter to clients and to fellow professionals, one's peers rather than one's superiors. There seems to have been a curious, hybrid period from the late eighteenth century to perhaps the 1860s, when schools and universities were quasi-bureaucracies. Organizational boundaries were not so encompassing as they have since become – either for staff or pupils. (In non-educational organizations the trend since the late Victorian period has probably been in a contrary direction, towards less encompassing boundaries. I think Bryan Wilson may be saying this, in the terminology of role, when, in a celebrated essay, he talks of the teacher-role becoming more diffuse and less affectively neutral precisely as other professional roles have become more specific and restricted.[12])

Before the middle of the nineteenth century both schools and universities were quasi-bureaucracies, providing a loose organizational structure within which semi-independent practitioners operated. The allegiance of teachers and university tutors was more to their clients than to their organization. Indeed, the greater part of their income was often from clients, in the form of fees, presents and even tips. Semi-independence of the school or college organization is one side of the picture; the other is ingratiation with pupils and their parents in the hope of a generous gratuity.

The headmaster of Eton had many of the characteristics of a head waiter until his position and salary were redefined and regularized after the report of the Clarendon Commission in 1864. In 1763 he received £411 in tips from his pupils and their parents. Annual gratuities were not obligatory, but parents saw the advantage of 'plentifully greasing the headmaster's palm'.[13] The Clarendon Commission found him in receipt of a gross income in excess of £6,000; his net income, after paying his eighteen assistants out of his own pocket, was £4,500. His statutory emoluments were only £375 per annum (and a rent-free house); he was making a further £5,700 from entrance fees, leaving presents, and annual payments by the boys. The commissioners recommended that he should have a fixed income of £4,000 per annum.

Until the later nineteenth century schools and colleges had members of staff incorporated and attached with widely varying degrees of commitment and obligation. Headmasters and other masters on the foundation were often virtually part-time appointments. John James, headmaster of Oundle from 1809 to 1829, received an income of £60 per annum. Extra subjects not prescribed by the foundation were taught by 'extra masters' who often made a good income from the fees they charged but were not incorporated in the school and had no position in the formal hierarchy. Foundation masters, who were usually paid to teach classical subjects, might also teach 'extra subjects', and charged fees for doing so. Some headmasters appear to have done nothing else.

It was possible for virtually autonomous, private-enterprise departments to be established within the framework of a school's general organization. Stephen Hawtrey established a private-enterprise mathematics department at Eton in 1837. He obtained a forty-year lease on a site in the college, built his own mathematical school in the form of a rotunda, a lecture-theatre which would accommodate 350 pupils, and recruited his own assistant mathematical masters. In 1851, after fourteen years in this endeavour, he persuaded the college authorities to make mathematics a compulsory subject (three hours a week). But he had been at Eton for nineteen years before he was officially recognized as a member of staff. His assistant mathematical masters never were.

Part-time commitment to their official duties was common among professors at Oxford and Cambridge in the middle of the nineteenth century. The stipends attached to professorships – like the emoluments of many headmasters – were insufficient in themselves. Giving evidence to the Royal Commission on Cambridge in 1852 Sir Henry Maine observed: 'It is virtually impossible that a professor should make the conduct of his faculty the principal occupation of his life. I myself am a practising barrister – my two immediate predecessors were beneficed clergymen.'[14]

Many tutors, both at public schools and at the ancient universities, had a tenuous and ambiguous relationship with the school or college. They were not simply semi-detached; they were wholly detached. They were fee-paid employees of students, and entirely outside the jurisdiction of the school or college. The tutorial system at Eton evolved from a practice of purely private tutoring by non-college personnel: 'In early days it was no uncommon thing for the sons of the great to bring with them to school a private tutor of their own.'[15]

The distinguishing feature of bureaucratic employment is a salary paid by the employing organization, as distinct from a fee paid directly to the practitioner by a client. An uneasy compromise between pre-bureaucratic and bureaucratic employment was evident at Eton as late as 1862, when the Royal Commission on the Public Schools was holding its inquiries. 'Extra teaching' was still given; the tutors were employees of the College; but the extent of such teaching and the amount paid for it was determined by private agreement with the parents. One Eton teacher described his (eminently gentlemanly) practice: 'I simply leave it to the parents. . . . I take simply what is given to me.'[16]

The bureaucratization of Oxford and Cambridge college tutors does not appear to have occurred until the early nineteenth century. Before this time a successful college fellow might attract numerous and wealthy students and so attain a position of considerable independence. His less successful colleagues were equally at the mercy of

D

college and clients. At St John's College, Cambridge, in 1565, there were 47 fellows of whom 5 were without pupils. Mostly they had 3 or 4; some had as many as 15. John Preston of Queens' College had 16 fellow-commoners and was referred to with some envy as 'the greatest pupil-monger in England in man's memory, having 16 fellow-commoners (most heirs to fair estates) admitted in one year at Queens' College'.[17] In its organization and discipline a college resembled an inn of court (I quote from a history of Balliol):

> The tutorial system was totally different [in the sixteenth century] from that which now prevails. A parent on bringing his son made his own choice of a tutor; the tutor undertook to look after the finances, the conduct, and the reading of a pupil, and stood to him *in loco parentis*; the fees were a matter of private agreement. From the outside point of view, the College was little more than a collection of 'coaches', who lived and compelled their charges to live under one roof. A minor result of the system, which is not without its bearing on the fortunes of the college, was that Fellows with a large connection were relatively independent of the Master and their colleagues; for they could always meet a threat of punishment for breaches of discipline with the counter-threat that they would carry off their clientele.[18]

Today the academic who has obtained large research funds from external sources may be in a similar position of power.

At Balliol the change to the present-day bureaucratic form of employment and organization was occurring in the later eighteenth century.

> In 1772–1773 the accounts show the payments of relatively substantial sums to three Fellows, presumably for tuition, for from 1780 the Fellows to whom such payments were made are called *tutores*. There is nothing in the Register to explain this innovation, but it may represent the change-over from the Elizabethan system of private arrangements between tutor and pupil (or his parents) to something like the nineteenth-century system of college tutors.[19]

The position of professors – especially underpaid regius professors – in the Scottish universities in the early nineteenth century well illustrates the problems and indignities attendant on pre-bureaucratic academic employment. The pre-bureaucratic professor was an

entrepreneur who fought rival teachers of his own subject as dangerous competitors and resisted the development of subjects closely
allied to his own, and the recognition of new subjects for graduation.
At Glasgow college professors received an average of £300 per
annum, regius professors £50.

> The greater part of a professor's income was often derived from
> class and examination fees which depended on the number of stu-
> dents. Clearly professors of recognized subjects enrolled large
> numbers of students, and were well paid in comparison with those
> in fringe disciplines. ... Personal interests were frequently hostile
> to change and encouraged recognized teachers to form con-
> servative groupings, keen to preserve their status and mon-
> opoly.[20]

Private teachers attracted students from university professors by
offering more attractive courses and charging lower fees. The universities had ill-defined organizational boundaries, affording inadequate
shelter for their members, who were obliged strenuously to fend for
themselves. The struggle for survival has been vividly told in the case
of Thomas Charles Hope, Professor of Chemistry and Medicine at
Edinburgh from 1799 to 1834. The University provided him with
little more than a title, and,

> like some of his medical colleagues at Edinburgh, [he] received
> neither salary nor capital and running expenses which he therefore
> met himself. Clearly he was heavily reliant on the fees paid by
> members of his class. An unsalaried professor like Hope depended
> on the financial rewards of gaining popularity with a large number
> of students. ... For many years Hope's emoluments were the high-
> est received by a professor in a Scottish university, his remuner-
> ation from class fees hovering around £2,000 a year. Given this
> sort of financial independence it is not surprising that professors
> tended to be monopolistic, jealously guarding their disciplines
> against both internal and external competition. Hope was no ex-
> ception in this regard: he allowed his tutorial assistant to use his
> apparatus for explanation but not for demonstration; and he re-
> garded the proposal made by the Scottish Universities Com-
> mission (1826), that medical students could attend private teachers
> for an imperative second course of chemistry, as a condemnation
> of his efficiency as well as an attack on his professorial rights.[21]

The independence of a fee-income is one side of the coin; the other, as a contemporary pointed out in 1830 in the *Quarterly Review*, is that such a professor 'is forced to become a commercial speculator, and under the dead weight of its degrading influence his original researches are either neglected or abandoned'.[22]

Rather loose collections of semi-independent practitioners were finally organized hierarchically in positions of defined super-ordination and subordination. This process is by no means clear, possibly because we approach it with naïve assumptions about the nature of authority and a zero-sum conception of power. Probably, all ranks gained in organizational power, while differences in rank became sharper. Precisely as headmasters became more powerful, so did their assistants.

Samuel Butler at Shrewsbury in the early decades of the nineteenth century illustrates the plight and powerlessness of the pre-bureaucratic head (especially in relation to his usher). Butler tried for thirty-seven years to control the teaching methods and disciplinary arrangements throughout his school and entirely failed to do so. Jendwine, the Second Master, regarded Butler's recommendations as 'interference' and continued in his own way. The early nineteenth-century headmaster was often in difficulty because he was principally a super-teacher; the modern headmaster is in difficulty because he is not.

Revised schemes of school government placed late Victorian headmasters in a more powerful position. They often attempted detailed regulation of their schools. T. C. Fry, appointed headmaster of Oundle in 1883, required staff to remain on school premises when they were not teaching and issued detailed, written instructions on teaching methods. Pugnacious and autocratic, he threw himself into his task with such zeal that he burned himself out in a year. During this brief period he fought housemasters and Old Boys and showed a businesslike efficiency which impressed the Governors. Appointed at thirty-seven, he retired with a nervous breakdown when he was thirty-eight.[23]

The power of assistant masters also increased. At least in the famous schools, men of high qualifications were recruited in the later nineteenth century, and their quality made them a power to be taken seriously. The reformed universities with their new honours schools were producing a much larger output of graduates of intellectual distinction. Many found careers in the restructured public and imperial service; but many more found their way into the schools. Between 1850 and 1880 the older universities, after remaining stationary in numbers for more than two centuries, doubled their numbers. In the thirty-seven years from 1850 to 1887 freshmen at Cambridge increased by 150 per cent.[24] The public school and grammar schools of late Victorian England were able to recruit from talented and able men.

James Wilson, headmaster of Clifton from 1879 to 1890, described his period of office as 'an age of great assistant masters'. Wilson was a practical administrator; he was not a great scholar, and his manner was didactic, but he ran a successful and efficient school. He was meticulous in his attention to detail. He attributed his success to his staff of exceptionally able men:

> I was astonished and uplifted at Clifton by the magnificent and helpful spirit of masters and boys. I cannot exaggerate this. It was a splendid staff of masters, some of whom were of quite exceptional ability. The school did what bees are said to do when they have accidentally lost their queen. They gather round an ordinary bee and make a queen of it.[25]

Henry Hayman at Rugby in the 1870s quite failed to appreciate the qualities and resourcefulness of his staff and within five years was driven from office. He was appointed in 1869 as Temple's successor. Temple judged him a self-willed and autocratic man 'who would never be able to work with the best type of assistant master'.[26] Even before he took up his appointment the assistant masters sent one of their number to demand that he withdraw from the headmastership. They had checked up on his testimonials and discovered that they were of doubtful reliability. (It is perhaps a sign of pre-bureaucratic appointment that personal recommendation, as distinct from formal qualifications, was still so very important. When Henry Montagu Butler applied – unsuccessfully – for Harrow in 1859 he supplied 31 testimonials from bishops and men of similar eminence; when Jex-Blake applied for Haileybury in 1867 he supplied 65 testimonials which were printed and bound in book form.)

Hayman took up his appointment and was immediately at loggerheads with his staff over elections to the new governing body and appointments to boarding houses. He ignored established custom in the matter of promotions and engaged in bitter conflict with the staff. He refused to assign pupils to A. E. Scott, whom he locked out of his classroom. Scott, with the help of the boys, took desks through the window and held his class in the Close. The final victory went to the assistant masters: after five embattled years, the Governors dismissed Hayman in 1874.

Bureaucracy means, above all, standardized procedures and standardized products. There are those who would say that, precisely for this reason, schools cannot be treated as bureaucracies.[27] I would maintain that it is precisely for this reason that they can. Yet, curiously, the standardization of human beings makes bureaucratic control and organizational loyalty less necessary. (Once again two features of bureaucracy are found in an inverse relationship to each other.) In schools we probably still insist on far more loyalty than our levels of standardization strictly require: we still demand loyalty of the order required by the great bureaucracies of history: the banking houses of Augsburg and Florence, the Jesuits, the Janissaries of the Ottoman Empire, the Prussian Grenadiers. Leaving was equivalent to treason[28] – as it was at Oundle in 1922 when the headmaster, Atkinson, was asked to resign because it became known that he was looking for another job. In spite of the picture drawn by Whyte in *The Organization Man*, the tendency this century has been for most bureaucracies to be less bureaucratic in this respect.

This is possible because standard replacements are readily available. When organizations depend on standard parts, and when standard parts are in plentiful supply, there is no need to insist on undeviating loyalty over forty years. In looking at the relationship between standardization and loyalty in the history of education, we lack good indicators of both. When Arthur Ponsonby wrote his *Decline of the Aristocracy* in 1912 he used school photographs to show how the public school product had become increasingly standardized over the previous half-century. He ascribed this process to the examination system which had grown up since the 1850s. In part he was right. But a deeper cause is probably the need of a more mobile society for readily interchangeable parts:[29] replacements can then be made without noticing the difference.

Contemporary studies of industrial organizations (for instance, by Joan Woodward[30] and by Burns and Stalker[31]) have shown how the standardization or otherwise of the product has consequences for the structure of authority. When the product is standardized, as in mass production, authority tends to be 'mechanistic' and hierarchical – and appropriately so, for maximum efficiency; but when the product is non-standardized, as in unit production, the organization is more likely to be 'organic', flexible and non-hierarchical. These hypotheses can be tested in the history of education over the past century. Research teams have a non-standardized, 'unreliable', indeed unpredictable product: their authority system is quite unlike that which produces a steady, reliable output of G.C.E. O-levels. And there is a further consequence of producing standard, predictable and reliable products: the organization's bargaining power with its environment is considerably weakened. It is at the mercy of the market.

In a short paper I have been able to touch only briefly on one or two of the features or dimensions of bureaucracy and the relationships between them. I have said nothing, for instance, about rules, and how their multiplication and formalization might be explored in relation to the growing social (and religious) heterogeneity of the pupil body, to school size, and above all, perhaps, to the stability of school numbers. Periods of rapid expansion make hierarchical authority difficult to maintain (a headmaster is judged by the proportion of his staff he can actually keep for more than a year); period of rapidly fluctuating numbers – as in the mid-nineteenth century – call for great organizational flexibility and adaptability. Fixed rules and regulations and a hierarchical chain of command depend on the expectation of recurrent and regular activities. We have good data on school numbers in the nineteenth century; we have done little to explore their significance for the organization of schools. Would inquiry support the hypothesis derived from contemporary studies (as well as from common sense) that authoritarian rule is easier under conditions of stability and established routine?[32] Victorian England provides a laboratory for the study of unstable schools.

I began by claiming that historical studies provide a basis for value-judgements. My judgement with regard to bureaucratization is this: that it has enormously reduced the average level of servility in society in general and in schools in particular. I would not hesitate to pronounce this a gain. The increase in human dignity has been incalculable. Servile governesses and tutors of the eighteenth century – many of the latter Fellows of the Royal Society – have been succeeded by self-confident and self-respecting teachers in comprehensive schools, with well-protected careers. (And if bureaucracy means subservience to rules, this is probably less humiliating than subservience to persons. A latter-day Joseph Priestley does not have to discover oxygen as an after-dinner entertainment for the Earl of Shelburne.) But bureaucracy has also meant a more standardized product, and the consequence is a more mechanistic and hierarchical authority within schools, and a weakened bargaining power for schools *vis-à-vis* the wider society. But, for my money, a significant average decline in servility is well worth it.[33]

Notes

1 E. H. Carr, *What Is History* (London: Macmillan, 1961).
2 J. H. Plumb, 'The Historian's Dilemma', in J. H. Plumb (ed.), *Crisis in the Humanities* (Harmondsworth: Pelican Books, 1964).
3 See M. Crozier, *The Bureaucratic Phenomenon* (London: Tavistock, 1964).
4 F. Musgrove, *The Family, Education and Society* (London: Routledge and Kegan Paul, 1966).
5 See Peter Laslett, *The World We Have Lost* (London: Methuen, 1965).
6 R. Bendix, *Work and Authority in Industry* (New York: John Wiley, 1956).
7 See Max Weber, *The Theory of Social and Economic Organization*, translated by A. M. Henderson and Talcott Parsons (New York: Oxford University Press, 1947).
8 R. H. Hall, 'The Concept of Bureaucracy: An Empirical Assessment', *American Journal of Sociology*, Vol. 69 (1963).
9 D. S. Pugh, D. J. Hickson, C. R. Hinings and C. Turner, 'Dimensions of Organization Structure', *Administrative Science Quarterly*, Vol. 13 (1968).
10 George Baron, 'Some Aspects of the "Headmaster Tradition"', *Researches in Education*, No. 14 (1956).
11 T. W. Bamford, *The Rise of the Public Schools* (London: Nelson, 1967).
12 B. R. Wilson, 'The Teacher's Role – A Sociological Analysis', *British Journal of Sociology*, Vol. 13 (1962).
13 G. F. Lamb, *The Happiest Days* (London: Michael Joseph, 1959), p. 104.
14 Quoted in Eric Ashby, 'The Academic Profession', *Minerva*, Vol. 8 (1970).
15 L. S. R. Byrne and E. L. Churchill, *Changing Eton* (London: Cape, 1937), p. 146.
16 Ibid., p. 148.
17 V. H. H. Green, *The Universities* (Harmondsworth: Penguin Books, 1969), p. 202.
18 H. W. Carless Davis, *A History of Balliol College* (Oxford: Blackwell, 1963), pp. 89–90.
19 Ibid., p. 274.

20 J. B. Morrell, 'Thomas Thompson: Professor of Chemistry and University Reformer', *British Journal of the History of Science*, Vol. 4 (1969).
21 J. B. Morrell, 'Practical Chemistry in the University of Edinburgh 1799–1843', *Ambix*, Vol. 16 (1969).
22 Quoted in ibid.
23 W. G. Walker, *A History of Oundle School* (London: Hazell, Watson and Viney, 1956).
24 A. I. Tillyard, *A History of University Reform* (Cambridge: C.U.P., 1913), p. 352.
25 James M. Wilson, *An Autobiography 1836–1931* (London: Sidgwick and Jackson, 1932).
26 Ibid., p. 80.
27 See J. D. Crambs, *Schools, Scholars and Society* (Englewood Cliffs, N.J.: Prentice-Hall, 1965), p. 159.
28 Cf. M. Crozier, op. cit.
29 Cf. F. Musgrove, *The Migratory Elite* (London: Heinemann, 1963).
30 See J. Woodward, *Management and Technology* (London: H.M.S.O., 1958).
31 See T. Burns and G. M. Stalker, *The Management of Innovation* (London: Tavistock, 1961).
32 Cf. B. J. Palisi, 'Some Suggestions about the Transitory-Permanence Dimension of Organizations', *British Journal of Sociology*, Vol. 21 (1970).
33 For a full treatment of the themes dealt with in this paper, see F. Musgrove, *Patterns of Power and Authority in English Education* (London: Methuen, 1971).

KENNETH CHARLTON

History and sociology: afterthoughts and prior questions

The purpose of this conference has been to examine the relationship between sociology and history. The question may be put rather more baldly. What is in mind, a co-operative venture, or a merger, or a take-over bid? Reading some of the contributions to the general debate elsewhere it seems to be the latter, for there are contributors[1] who have claimed that the study of history (and thereby the study of history of education) is necessarily inadequate unless and until it is studied in a sociological manner, using the techniques, concepts and theoretical frameworks of the sociologist. Nor would they count a piece of writing as 'good' history, unless it was written in this way, unless it could be called 'sociological history'.[2]

But this is to put the matter too simply, to put the cart before the horse, to beg the prior question which has yet to be posed, and which is this: are the concepts, techniques and theoretical orientations of sociology (useful as they may have been to sociologists) of similar use to the historian, appropriate to the evidence available to the historian, and compatible with the basic assumptions of the historian? We have to ask not only what is to be the relationship between history and sociology, but also the prior question, is a relationship possible at all?

I take it to be axiomatic that in principle the work of historians can be illuminated by a variety of other disciplines, and in fact this has already taken place. Philosophy, for example, has at least encouraged historians to examine and clarify the assumptions on which they base their work and the logical status of the explanations they offer. Similarly psychology has reminded historians of the complexity of human nature and of human behaviour, and, to take a particular example, of the characteristics of crowd behaviour. We need, then, to ask ourselves in what ways (if any) do the concepts and techniques of sociology illuminate the work of a historian? And in order to answer this we have to seek the answers to further questions: which concepts? which techniques? and how far are these characteristically and peculiarly sociological? For example, when Musgrave talks about 'such new concepts as social mobility'[3] how far is such a phenomenon 'new' to historians and how far is the concept characteristically sociological? The final question, then, will be: given that these concepts and techniques can be identified, given that they have been developed in the study of sociology, are they then appropriate to or compatible with the study of history, which having its own concepts and techniques has not only its own conceptual difficulties, its own technical difficulties, but also its own basic assumptions and prior premisses?

The traditional mode of explanation of the historian (if by that is meant some principle of coherence which will enable the historian to answer his own characteristic forms of the question 'why?', i.e. why did an event happen as it did when it did? How did it come to happen as it did when it did? How did the persons involved come to act as they did when they did?) is by narrative. That is the historian so arranges his data that their very chronologicality gives them a coherence they would not otherwise have had. But few historians today would claim that this mode of explanation is a sufficient one; a necessary part of historical explanation maybe, but not sufficient in itself, not allowing for a sufficient explanation of the complexity of human relationships. The sociologist claims that he has in his own work developed a mode of explanation which would improve on this.

One difficulty, however, is to determine what is the sociological approach, what techniques and concepts and theoretical frameworks are distinctively sociological. It would clear the ground, I suppose, if we were to discount first of all those meta-sociologists who sought laws with a level of generality which matched those of the physical scientists; i.e. those 'necessitarian' sociologists according to whom 'no decisions of a group of persons can, given the existing state of affairs, prevent the predictable successive states from coming into existence'. May we take it that, nowadays, sociologists do not seek universally inclusive explanations of the 'covering law' kind? If we (and they) do, we then have to ask why and in what sense(s) they continue to use the word 'theory'. We know, of course, that, no longer seeking after general laws, they are content with 'theories of the middle range'.[4] But how non-general is 'middle', and what then is the status of terms such as 'theoretical frameworks', 'observed regularities', 'meaningful similarities', 'recurrent patterns', 'typical developmental sequences' and so on, with which the sociologists concern themselves and from which, even so, it is claimed that predictions can be made. A further difficulty arises from the sociologists' undifferentiated use of terms such as 'law', 'theory', 'general principle', 'model' and 'hypothesis', a usage nowhere more apparent, unfortunately, than in the Introduction to Musgrave's collection of readings for students, where we also find that 'it is with universal hypotheses ... that theoretical disciplines like sociology are largely concerned'.[5]

These are difficulties which need to be cleared up before the substantive part of the debate can begin, but before we go any further perhaps we could also agree to eschew those dichotomizing lists which say, for example:

—that whilst the historian is interested in individuals, the socio- ist is interested in individuals only in so far as they typify groups of individuals.
—that whilst history is a particularizing discipline, sociology is a generalizing discipline.
—that whilst the sociologist is self-consciously theoretical, the historian is innocent of such ambitions.
—that whilst the historian adopts the stance of methodological individualism, the sociologist embraces holism, organicism, scientism.
—that whilst sociologist's aims are nomothetic, the historian's are idiographic.

If we were to abandon such simplifications, however, we would still have to decide in what respects (if any) the historian's assumptions about his work and the subject-matter of his work differ from those of the sociologist. It cannot be simply (yet another dichotomy) that whilst the historian is interested in the past, the sociologist is interested in the present. For whilst the historian may not necessarily be interested in the present, the sociologist is very definitely interested in both. Yet if we concentrate on their joint interest in the past this does not necessarily mean that they both study the past using the same methods, for the same purposes, with the same assumptions. The difference in their studies must then lie in their approach to the past, in their approach to past events and personalities, and particularly in their means of explaining past events and in their willingness to offer generalizations about them.

Neil Smelser says that sociological explanation consists in 'bringing constructs such as hypotheses, models and theories to bear on factual statements'.[6] What is the historian to say to this? Merely that he does not simply collect data at random, that he has some principles of selection to which he might rather sheepishly apply the label 'hypotheses'. But he does not then proceed to test or falsify these in any 'scientific' way. Rather he uses them to guide his search, so that he can roughly determine what is relevant and what is not relevant for the illumination of the problematical question which confronts him, or rather of the problematical question which he has posed of a particular time and place. His hypothesis will guide him in answering his first question, 'What actually happened?' And if he is content to be a narrative historian he will then write his history as a series of chronologically connected events. If he goes beyond this to ask 'Why did it happen?' he will make it clear that he is not seeking a strictly causal explanation in the terms of either logic or natural science–'if p then q' . . . 'if C then E', where the one is related to the other in a strictly necessary manner. Nor if he is wise does he try to explain by reference to some Immanent Will or First Cause. He is first and last concerned to ask 'Why did men act as they did when they did?' and he will base his explanation on the assumption (and it is only an assumption) that the relationship between events is a contingent one, that events happen which could have happened quite differently. In other words, it is for the historian to *show* the relationship, which is not a relationship of entailment. The historian's work rests on an assumption that though the choices open to the people of the past did not extend beyond a limited range of behaviour they were free to make choices. As Herbert Butterfield has put it, 'nobody is to be explained as the mere product of his age'.[7] For the historian no amount of 'role theory', for example, will alter the fact that, though individuals act within limited possibilities, the contingency of the situations allows not only for a variety of possible actions, but for idiosyncratic action or even for no action at all. When as historians of education we consider the role of the teacher in the sixteenth century we have immediately to think in terms not only of the roles of the teacher, nor indeed only of what others counted the roles of the teacher to be, but in addition – if we are to write *history* – in terms of identifying for a given time and a given place what roles individual teachers believed they *ought* to have, irrespective of what others considered their roles should be. Nor is this all, for however precisely we formulate our questions none of this will lead us to a truth about 'the role of the teacher in the sixteenth century'.

The contingency of the situation is not, therefore, denied simply by recognizing a limitation on the choices open to a particular actor. In other words to consider some event historically is to admit the possibility that it *may* not have occurred as it did when it did, and indeed may not have occurred at all. It is its specific connection with other events, not its general connection with other events, which makes an event interesting to the historian. So that when a historian studies (and seeks to explain) the influences of Rousseau's educational writings on the English and German Romantics he does so on the assumption that, though some individual Englishmen and Germans reacted positively to Rousseau's writings, they could have chosen to do the reverse, and others in fact did. The historian insists, therefore, that human beings are the only moving agents in history. 'Social tendencies', 'typical developmental sequences' and so on are very strictly the product of characteristically human activities – and it is not sufficient merely to retort, as Holloway does for example, that historians generalize anyway.[8] For though they use generic terms they do not use them as a base from which predictions might be made. Though they use the general term 'battle' to refer to Hastings, Lepanto and Waterloo they do not go on to seek either a general covering law or a theory of the middle range in order to explain why each took place as it did when it did. It would, I suppose, be possible to make a comparative study of all the battles of history and come up with a classification (even one a little more sophisticated than land, sea and air) but it would not, I think, be counted as a *historical* study. For historians are well aware that all too often and all too easily 'discernible regularities' become impersonal and activating 'social forces'.

With these points in mind, then, let us turn now to the sociologist's search for precision. This has two objects: a conceptual precision and a statistical precision, which we might look at in turn. The value of conceptual precision, as Mr Bernbaum reminded us when he quoted R. K. Merton, is that 'it serves as a control over the introduction of unrelated, undisciplined and diffuse interpretations. It does not impose upon the reader the task of ferreting out the relations between the interpretations embodied in the text.'[9] The crucial word here, of course, is 'control', and the historian would want to ask what degree of control a concept or a model or a theory is meant to have over the historical data he has available to him. Such prior conceptualization may very well lead the historian to look for some feature or other in his chosen historical situation which he might otherwise have overlooked, but this is a far cry from 'control', from the 'application' of a theory or model or concept, especially when the sociologist tries to apply to particularly mobile and complex materials and situations concepts, etc., which ordinarily presuppose materials and situations of a much more constant and static kind.

We might take as an example the sociologist's attitude to the word 'period'. As Musgrave puts it, 'to characterize a given stretch of time in such a way is to make a hypothesis that there is an important and identifiable break with the flow of history'.[10] But in fact historians use the term not only differentially, but with a due awareness that it is a relatively unsophisticated heuristic device, a label or shorthand term which may be used in a relatively descriptive way, as for example when the term 'Tudor period' is used to mean 'those years during which a member of the Tudor family was on the throne', and in an extremely dangerous and misleading way as when some one person or idea is characterized as being 'typically Tudor', which is precisely what the sociologist is looking for. The historian, on the other hand, would not go to the trouble of attempting a scientific categorization or even a philosophical characterization and certainly not a sociological 'ideal-type' definition, for he knows of what limited use such definitions would be to him. Nevertheless, knowing this, he still uses the term. With all its limitations he finds it a useful, shorthand label. Precisely because he is aware of its limitations he is able to use it for limited purposes. It is, as the sociologists would say, an 'auxiliary construct', which must not, however, be used to impose typological patterns on the diverse and partial evidence we have of human life and behaviour in the past. Examples of the ways in which such constructs have become reality in the minds of men are Rostow's stages of economic growth and Piaget's stages of child development.

A similar claim to conceptual precision is made when another sociologist writes that 'the terms sect and denomination have been refined by successive sociologists into valuable weapons of analysis'.[11] What the claim really amounts to is that sociologists have offered successive stipulative definitions of these terms – a matter of semantics and logic, not of sociology. If this activity reminds the historian of the differentiated usage of these words, well and good, but he must beware of imposing his stipulations on his material at

the expense of determining how the words were used by the people of
the past and what significance the words had for them.

But there is a further danger in this search for conceptual precision, and it might be illustrated by reference to a recent article by
two sociologists entitled 'Dominance and Assertion: Towards a
Theory of Educational Change'. 'The following theory', they write,
'has been developed in connection with a study of educational
change in England and France from 1800 to 1850', which seems to
me to be a very middle-range theory indeed, and yet which gives
forth the generalization (presumably valid for other half-centuries)
that

> ... prolonged educational stability corresponds to the lasting
> domination of a particular group. However it is not synonymous
> with the absence of conflict, merely with the successful use of
> social control. While educational conflict does not necessarily
> imply that a dominant group is challenged by an assertive one,
> educational change results from the successful assertion of a group
> against an existing form of domination. It is therefore by inves-
> tigating the main pre-requisites of successful domination and as-
> sertion that one can account for educational stability and
> change.[12]

Here, it seems to me, the search for precise conceptualization which
will nevertheless allow of widely inclusive generalization has led the
authors of the article inexorably along the road to highly generalized
triviality.

Indeed it is by no means an indubitable point that sociologists use
a more precise language than historians. I wonder, for example, how
much more precise the sociologist's 'truce situation' is than the historian's 'compromise' or 'coalition'. And how precise in his com-
munication of ideas is another sociologist when, writing of that other
sociological concept 'the definition of the situation', he explains that
'The system as a system-maintaining or determining activity,
which operates in terms of adaptation, integration, tension-manage-
ment and pattern-maintenance of shared norms and values'?[13]

I cannot deal in detail here with the sociologist's search for
statistical precision. As I examine their exhortations, however, I take
it that they would not be satisfied with mere arithmetic, with mere
head-counting – I think Mr Bernbaum called it 'aggregation' –
though this is what Lawrence Stone does, and this is what many

historically inclined sociologists do when they study literacy levels in the nineteenth century. Yet, having carefully indicated the inadequacies of their data-source, they nevertheless go on to subject their data to sophisticated and rigorous statistical treatment; in other words persisting in their ambitions to construct literacy indices to two points of decimals in the face of the acknowledged unreliability of their historical evidence. When, to refer to another field, one regards the pathetic little graphs (all two of them) in Kearney's *Scholars and Gentlemen*[14] one blushes for the seduction not of the innocent but of those who ought to know better. Peter Laslett, of course, is batting on a much better wicket, for when he quantifies infant mortality, expectation of life, chances of women being pregnant at marriage, rate of illegitimacy, size of families and the rather more sophisticated phenomenon of age-specific fertility, he uses a mass of reliable evidence *which is susceptible of quantification*. Whether in doing this, he is 'doing' history or sociology or demography is a moot point, which would require the stating of prior premises before an answer would be forthcoming.

We have then to scrutinize a claim which has a positive and a negative side. The positive side of the claim insists that by 'bringing to bear' on the evidence of the past a previously formulated conceptual framework of theory and a set of statistical techniques sociologists can produce a variety of *history* which is superior to that currently produced and which may be called sociological history. Moreover, this is not to be regarded simply as a new *content* area of history, to put alongside the traditional political history, religious history, history of art and so on, but rather as the application of a sophisticated coherent *method* which is called 'sociological', and which can and should be applied to all content areas of history, not least of which is history of education. The negative side of the claim asserts that history (including history of education) is not *good* history unless it uses this particular methodological approach.

These are claims which are made in all seriousness, and we have therefore to take them seriously. If, as Mr Bernbaum claims, sociologists have drawn the attention of historians to areas of study not hitherto the major concern of historical study – 'occupational structure, social stratification, the family and the whole kinship order ... social mobility',[15] to say nothing of Professor Musgrove's 'bureaucratization of schools',[16] then it would be churlish of the historian to deny his indebtedness. A real difference of opinion arises, however, if the sociologist then goes on to insist that the historian should study these topics sociologically, should base his work on characteristically sociological assumptions about human behaviour. In the same way, no historian can, in conscience, reject the sociologist's reminder of the need for a greater quantitative precision when he ventures into a quantifiable field, though he may well point out that the sociologist has no monopoly of this virtue, which is neither original nor peculiar to sociology.

But a concentration on these two aspects of the debate has led some to urge that these are really the only differences between the two disciplines, that if only historians would wake up, enlarge their horizons beyond their traditional areas of study and at the same time become more precise in their conceptualizing and their quantifying then the difference would disappear. This, however, is to imply that the two disciplines share the same basic assumptions, to the same degree and with the same purposes in mind, and this, I would argue, is very far from being the case, for despite my earlier comments about dichotomies, the basic assumptions of the two disciplines are separated by a great logical gulf, which no amount of technique refinement will bridge – any more than the increasingly efficient and precise way in which psychologists conceptualized and measured 'intelligence' enabled them to reconcile conflicting basic assumptions about the nature of what they were measuring.

The exponents of our two disciplines (and I choose my words carefully here – I am not referring to abstract entities called 'history' and 'sociology') choose to start their work from two quite distinct assumptions about the 'lawfulness' of human behaviour past and present, two quite distinct assumptions about the susceptibility of human behaviour to description and explanation by reference to generalized statements of such relative precision that predictions can be made from them. The sociologist, I take it, starts from the assumption that there is a 'lawfulness', that behaviour may be described and explained in terms of statements which have a *general* applicability to other situations and persons. The historian, however, will start with the assumption that though this *may* be the case in certain situations it is not necessarily the case. He starts, as I said, with the *contingent* nature of human behaviour.

The sociologist may claim virtue in the precision with which he works, and he may rightly and justly criticize the historian if he is not as precise as he could be, but this is not to say that the historian should at the same time abandon his basic assumptions. This is a take-over bid, not even a merger, still less a mutual exchange of ideas. The sociologist's line is 'Look what I've done – go thou and do likewise' – and the historian can only accede by doing something other than history. In other words there is a real possibility of a contradiction in terms in the phrase 'sociological history', if it is to be used in any precise way. As Orlo Williams has put it, 'Theories are like omnibuses, useful when you want to go in the same direction but not otherwise.'

This situation is of course no new one, for when new and exciting techniques and methodologies are developed which produce satisfying results in a limited area with particular kinds of data, there is a tendency on the part of some articulate and enthusiastic practitioners to apply their new-found skills across the board, with little regard for relevance, applicability, appropriateness. When this happens it enables a psychologist, for example, to write of Hannah More: 'psycho-analysis in emphasizing the subjective aspects of her life's work interprets it in terms of anal eroticism, patrism-matrism, unconscious as well as manifest guilt and aggression, and the relative rigidity of ego-boundaries.'[17]

The other danger which seems implicit in the sociologist's claim is that what is not precisely formulated in terms of a conceptualized model is not worth bothering about. In insisting on being so self-consciously theoretical the sociologist is in danger of losing contact with the world of men and women, their doubts, their fears, their aspirations and their follies, and on occasion their plain cantankerousness, if not bloodymindedness, in their determination to avoid doing the expected thing.

May I conclude, then, with a note of warning. It is by no means original, but it nevertheless loses nothing by repetition. The hope which originally inspired the concept of methodology was the hope of finding a method of inquiry which would be both necessary and sufficient to guide the inquirer unerringly to the truth. It is a hope which springs eternal – which is all the more reason to remind ourselves that methodology can bear only a modest burden, that of establishing certain rules and requirements which inquirers place upon themselves as self-denying ordinances, which are necessary to prevent some wrong-headed moves on the part of the inquirer, but are insufficient to guarantee success.

Notes

1 e.g. S. W. F. Holloway, 'Sociology and History', *History*, N.S., Vol. XLVIII (1963), pp. 154–80, and 'History and Sociology: What History is and What it Ought to be', in W. H. Burston and D.Thompson (eds.), *Studies in the Nature and Teaching of History* (London: Routledge and Kegan Paul, 1967).

2 Musgrave seems to make no distinction between 'sociological history' and 'historical sociology': 'From this process of using historical material and doing historical research is born the true [*sic*] "historical sociology" or "sociological history".' P. W. Musgrave, *Sociology, History and Education: A Reader* (London: Methuen, 1970), p. 9.

3 Ibid., p. 3.

4 Cf. R. K. Merton, *Social Theory and Social Structure* (Chicago: Free Press, 1957), and 'On Sociological Theories of the Middle Range', in his collection of essays, *On Theoretical Sociology* (New York: Free Press, 1967).

5 Musgrave, op. cit., p. 3.

6 N. J. Smelser, *Essays in Sociological Explanation* (New Jersey: Prentice-Hall, 1968), p. 58.

7 H. Butterfield, 'The Role of the Individual in History', *History*, N.S., Vol. XL, Nos. 138–9 (February–June 1955), p. 4.

8 Holloway, 'Sociology and History', p. 154.

9 G. Bernbaum, 'Sociology and Contemporary History', *Educational Review*, Vol. 20, No. 3 (June 1968), p. 198.

10 Musgrave, op. cit., p. 8.

11 E. A. Isichei, 'From Sect to Denomination in English Quakerism, with Special Reference to the Nineteenth Century', *British Journal of Sociology*, Vol. XV (1964), p. 207.

12 M. S. Archer and M. Vaughan, 'Domination and Assertion: Towards a Theory of Educational Change', *European Archives of Sociology*, Vol. IX (1968), p. 2.

13 C. M. Turner, 'Sociological Approaches to the History of Education,' *British Journal of Educational Studies*, Vol. XVII, No. 2 (June 1969), p. 147.

14 H. Kearney, *Scholars and Gentlemen: Universities and Society in Pre-Industrial Britain 1500–1700* (London: Faber, 1970), pp. 40–1 and 56–7.

15 G. Bernbaum, see above p. 7.

16 F. Musgrove, see above pp. 33 ff.

17 John McLeish, *Evangelical Religion and Popular Education: A Modern Interpretation* (London: Methuen, 1969), p. 131.

Index

aggregative method of studying population, 10
analysis, unconscious, of historian, 5
Aronson, Sidney M., 15
assistant masters, era of great, 43–4
authority
  effect of rapid expansion on, 45
  effect of standardization on, 44–6
auxiliary construct, 54
Aydelotte, W. O., 5

Bamford, T. W., 37
Banks, J. A., 6
Banks, O., 11
Baron, George, 37
Bendix, R., 34
Bernbaum, G., 53, 56
Bernstein, Basil, 18
Board of Education, employment by patronage at, 25
boarding schools, interviews of applicants for Civil Service from, 29–30
Bottomore, T. B., 4
bureaucracy
  dimensions of, 36, 45
  following internal self-government, 35
  operation and consequencs of, 33
  standardization as corollary of, 44, 46
  value-judgement of educational, 33, 45–6
bureaucratic employment, distinguishing feature of, 39
bureaucratization
  indicated in ratio between support and front-line personnel, 34
  of employment in schools, 33, 42–4, 56
  in universities, 39–40, 42
Burns, T., 44
Butler, Samuel, headmaster of Shrewsbury, 42
Butterfield, Sir Herbert, 52

Cambridge
  Royal Commission on, 39

University, examinations favouring applicants from, 24–5, 31
  pre- and quasi-bureaucratic employment in, 38–40
Carr, E. H., 33
centralization in organization of education, 36–7
Cicourel, A. V., 1
Civil Service Commission, 23, 32
  examinations for selection by intellectual capacity only, 23–6
  breached by interview, 27–31
  breached by Method II, 31–2
Clarendon Commission, 37–8
  schools, advantages of viva examinations to applicants from, 29–30
classification of sociology, 4
classificatory generalizations, historical, 5, 63
Clifton School, great assistant masters at, 43
comparative method, sociological, 17
concepts
  historical, in understanding social structure, 2
  of sociology, development of, 4
conceptual precision, sociological search for, 53–5
construct, auxiliary, 54
content analysis
  of documents, 9
  of war propaganda, 10
contingency of events, historical assumption of, 52, 57
control of interpretations, 4, 53
covering law, general, 50, 53
Crozier, M., 33–4
cruelty to children, improvement in, 34

day schools, interviews of applicants for Civil Service from, 29–30
definition of the situation, 55
democracy, relationship between bureaucracy and, 35
demography, historical, 10
documents
  content analysis of, 9